W9-BSV-345

DADDY, I'M PREGNANT

One Family's Story of Turning Tragedy into Triumph

DADDY, I'M PREGNANT

One Family's Story of Turning Tragedy into Triumph

Author: A dad named Bill

COLLEGE PRESS
PUBLISHING COMPANY
Joplin, Missouri

Copyright 1987 Multnomah Press
Expanded edition © 1998 College Press Publishing Co.

Library of Congress Cataloging-in-Publication Data

Dad named Bill
   Daddy, I'm pregnant: one family's story of turning tragedy
into triumph / "a dad named Bill."
    p. cm.
  Originally published: Portland, Or.: Multnomah Press,
c1987.
  ISBN 0-89900-800-3 (pbk.)
  1. Teenage mothers—United States—Case studies.
  2. Teenage pregnancy—United States—Case studies.
  3. Family—Religious life—Case studies. I. Title.
HQ759.4.D32 1998
306.8'7—dc21   97-50108
                                         CIP

To our Heavenly Father, to my wife and children
and our extended family . . .
To the church that gave us grace when we needed it . . .
To little Ashley . . . in our hands but a moment,
in our hearts for a lifetime.
To Angela, who taught us you can't go back,
but because of Jesus Christ you can start over.

Preface

From the moment I heard my fourteen-year-old daughter say, "Daddy, I'm pregnant!" I knew God would be stretching me beyond anything I'd ever experienced.

But at that moment God helped me to hold her ever so tight, and I was able to forgive her and tell her I loved her. I woke up the rest of the family and we cried and prayed together. As my wife Bobbi and I held each other through the remainder of that endless night, we let the Lord bind us together for the coming emotional storms.

The next morning we took Angela to the doctor to verify her pregnancy. Then Bobbi and I went to our trusted friends for counsel; they encouraged us to think through our options carefully.

At lunch we helped Angela make a list of those who

needed to be told she was pregnant. Then we went to the office to call those special people. As her dad I told them the news. Every one of them expressed sorrow and asked, "How is Angela? Tell her I love her." I said, "Here, I'll let you tell her yourself." Then we sat with her as she called her friends. It wasn't easy, but she managed.

I felt I needed to concentrate on being the best father and husband I could be, so I found someone to preach for me on Sunday. Those extra hours with the family were vital to me.

I asked Angela what she thought she had to do to get right with God. I am so glad she wanted to step forward in church and confess her sin, asking God and the church to forgive her.

I then called for a special meeting of the church leaders so they could give me counsel. They needed to decide how to respond to Angela's statement of repentance and how to decide whether or not they wanted my resignation. They were wonderful.

The family sat with Angela during the church service, and as she stepped forward to confess her sin, Bobbi and I stepped forward to stand with her. We watched as the leaders of the church came to stand with her. We listened as the spokesman said, "I know Angela has sinned, but because she has repented and asked God's forgiveness, we believe God has forgiven her, and we, the leaders of the church, stand before you to say that we have forgiven her and we want you also to forgive her."

After church, I called Dan (the baby's father) on the phone to make an appointment with his parents. I told them, "My wife and I believe you are good parents, and we know that we have done everything we could to be good parents, but our children have chosen to go against what we have taught them. Could we get together and talk about how we are going to help the kids with their problem?"

We went to Dan's home and I asked to speak with him privately. I told him I forgave him and that I wanted to help him with his hurts and disappointments. I explained that I needed his cooperation and asked him to commit himself to stand by our daughter until the baby was born.

We explained to his parents that we knew there would be future decisions, but that for now we just wanted this first meeting to weld us into a support team to help our children face the future.

What about the future?

The Lord was with us. His presence gave us the needed strength to survive the day, but how would we face tomorrow? A day at a time, a step at a time.

So many questions filled our minds; what should we decide to do?

Our faith and conviction that life begins at conception eliminated abortion. Others might be able to live with this possibility, but neither we nor Angela could accept this as an option. So many questions . . . so much unknown, it was mind boggling.

Should our fourteen-year-old daughter marry that fifteen-year-old boy?

Should Angela keep the baby and raise it as a single parent?

Should Bobbi and I take the child and raise it as our own?

Should we pray for a Christian family who would adopt the child and love it as their own?

Will our little daughter be safe through the birth of the child?

Will she and Dan marry sometime in the future?

Will his parents become our friends?

What about finances?

How will Angela's example affect the other children in our home?

Has Angela learned the lesson that you must love God more than you love any boy?

How will she be treated by the kids at school?

What will happen to the baby?

What will happen to my position as a Christian leader?

Time would answer many of these questions. In time, with God's help, comfort and healing would come.

This book is a collection of my journal entries through the nine months of our daughter's pregnancy. It is personal in nature and was never intended to be published. But I remember how desperately my wife and I searched for something to read and found nothing. It is my prayer that as you read this little journal, you will see the care and faithfulness of God to one family, and in the broader sense, His faithfulness to all who call on His name.

In Christ,

A dad named Bill

August

August 1

"DADDY, I'M PREGNANT, I'M SORRY, I'M SO SORRY . . .
PLEASE DON'T HATE ME!"

Only twelve words and yet they knocked the breath right out of me. Today is Saturday. At 2:30 a.m. my sobbing daughter burst into my bedroom, and I will never forget the words that awakened me . . .

"Daddy, I'm pregnant . . ."

My daughter Angela. I helped deliver her into this world, and from the time she could walk she was one of my five children who came into my room every night and kissed me good night. She was the one child who just couldn't stay overnight with friends or make it through a whole week at church camp without feeling homesick. She was our one child who just couldn't stand it if she didn't feel close to her parents.

For some weeks I had felt as if she were missing. She no longer shared her heart with me. She no longer laughed or cried with me. She never left physically, but the closeness we had always felt was gone. Week after week I spent time praying for her and asking her to come talk with me. But night after night her eyes were cold and her mouth was silent . . . *my daughter was missing* . . . and at 2:30 a.m. on a Saturday morning, I found out why.

I have gone through periods of time when I have had to act simply by faith because my emotions cried out, "Lord, are you really there?"

But in the middle of the night, when anger and condemnation could have slipped from my lips, I felt love for my daughter . . . the right words came from my mouth . . . the right thoughts as to what course of action to take came to my mind. In a second, peace filled my heart, and in spite of the circumstances, I sensed God's presence.

When Angela cried, "Daddy, I'm pregnant!" my arms reached out to take her in and from my mouth came the words, "Oh Angela, I'm so sorry . . . I love you! I forgive you."

During the rough, uncertain days ahead I wanted Angela to remember that no matter what the future held, I would always love her, stand by her, and protect her. Of course I had told her that before, but it seemed wise to put it in writing — something she could pick up and hold in her hands and read . . .

Dear Angela,

This has been a long and difficult day. Your news in the middle of the night and the many decisions we have had to make have blurred my mind. I have a very heavy heart and I need God's comfort.

Of all the many things I said today . . . the mini-sermons, the statements reminding you of past "sermons," I pray the one thing you remember is that your mother and I love you.

There are some things I feel I must say to you as you face the future. I am not proud of what you have done. I am hurt. I can see that what you have done will cause some people to no longer trust my leadership. But, depending on how our family handles this, there may be others who will be helped by our experience.

I want to shake you . . . and hug you. I want to spank you . . . and hold you in my arms. I want to do all this because I love you.

I don't know what the future will hold. I do know that unless you truly repent before the Lord, the soft tender girl I've always known will become a hard unhappy woman. I know that your failure will either be turned over to the Lord or you will fail again in the future.

I have watched the family rally around you. I loved seeing Joani and Melissa act like protective loving sisters. I enjoyed seeing Melody ask me if she could go to your room and tell you she loved you. It was neat to see Jim struggle with the typical older brother reaction to strangle you and the boy, yet finally manage to express his love to you.

I've watched your mother struggle to contain her emotions because she wanted so much to be helpful and not hurtful.

This has been a wonderfully difficult day. Today we acted as a family. Today you were the one who received the family's love and care. Sometime in the future, when God has healed your heart and taught you to care more for him and for the family than you care for yourself, you will be able to repay what you have received. When others in the family fail in some way, you too can become one through whom God will give his grace.

You have said that on Sunday you want to walk down the aisle at church and confess your sin, asking people to pray for you. I cannot guarantee how others will respond, but I know that God will receive you back and that your family will stand beside you.

Tonight Dan will arrive back from camp and you will have to tell him the news. He will have to muster the courage you did this morning and tell his parents. I'm not filled with hate for Dan. I understand

13

that what happened occurred because you loved each other. But Sis, please understand that when you love each other more than God, this kind of sin will occur. You have sinned. You have sought God's forgiveness, you have asked for our forgiveness. Your mother and I have forgiven you. What you must learn from this is that you must ask for forgiveness and then go on. One step at a time will lead us over this problem. We will find forgiveness but we will never find forget-fulness. We can't forget, so we must learn from the problem.

What does the future hold? It holds many hurts, memories, and frus-trations. It also holds the grace of God and the love of your family.

I love you,

Dad

Lord, thanks for being with me. There are so many emo-tions I could have felt. I could have been overwhelmed by the fear of losing my job or having to resign. I could have demand-ed, "Why, God?" or I could have been ashamed and started doubting my worth as a father. I could have blamed the boy or been fearful of telling the church. I could have yelled at Angela, "You are no longer my daughter!"

By ourselves we might have been completely out of con-trol. Thanks for helping us to be adequate to face the pressures of this difficult day. It has been a joy to see my family rely on you. Thanks for never being more than a breath away.

August 2

The news of the pregnancy is out. Family, friends, the people at church all know, and they have been wonderful. The grace they have shown has made it possible to move past the embarrassment and self-doubt to confront the real issues.

Angela has bravely faced every day with a mixture of tears and resolve. I have watched a little girl, who placed too much emphasis on what her friends thought, stand firm in her faith. With trembling chin, she faced the consequences of her sin.

This week I said to her, "Angela, I have a new definition for courage."

"What's that, Daddy?"

"You," I replied.

During the first week several things happened that are worth remembering:

Friends called to express concern, to give counsel, and to hold us up. Some of the friends I thought would call didn't, and some friends I thought really didn't care called to assure us of their love.

Realizing that nothing travels faster than "bad news," I asked my daughter Joani, "Who is the biggest gossip in the high school?" She named her.

"Call her and tell her about Angela. School will start soon, and by the time it does I want the kids to be talking about something else."

Thursday evening I was feeling very empty. Melody and I were the only ones home. I knew that if I stayed home the phone would ring, and even though I should be out calling, I just couldn't bring myself to go. How could I minister to others when I was hurting so myself?

A wonderful thing happened. On the night Angela told the family about her pregnancy, Melody had stayed overnight with a friend so she felt very left out.

"Melody, how about you and I going to see the movie 'E.T.'?" She replied with a quick "Okay" and off we went.

I couldn't concentrate on the movie. My thoughts and emotions were going wild. I had been in control every minute of the last six days. I had been bigger than I am — more under control than I could possibly be. So, after the movie I just fell apart. I could hardly see to drive. Great sobs came from deep within, and it was in that precious moment that God used Melody to help me.

That little girl, who felt so left out because she had not been home the night Angela told the family, was being used by God to bring comfort to my heart. As long as I live, I'll never forget her words.

"It's all right, Dad. I haven't had a good cry yet either. It's great to be able to be real and cry." God used Melody to help me through the most difficult moment I had faced so far.

August 4

One of the special blessings in this entire situation is the effect the pregnancy has had on our nineteen-year-old son. When Angela broke the news I fully expected Jim to react out of hurt and humiliation and to cause major problems. When he was told that his sister had decided to step forward in church and confess her sin, he went to her in private and said, "I can't go to church tomorrow because I just can't cry in public, but I want you to know I love you."

He stayed with a friend on the weekend, and on Monday he called from work asking Angela and Dan if they would go to a movie with him. I nearly passed out! Is this the same brother who said he would kill anyone who touched one of his sisters? And now he was asking them to go to a movie with him!

When Jim picked up Dan at his home, his dad called from the porch, "Well, son, come back alive!"

After the movie, as they pulled into Dan's driveway, Jim said, "I want you to know that I respect how you two have handled this so far. I want you to know that Mom and Dad, the rest of the family, and the church can forgive you this ONCE, but if this ever happens again, or if you don't accept responsibility for what's going on I'll kick your rears."

Jim continued, "I don't know if you are going to marry my sister, but if you stand with her through the birth of the child, I'll be the first one to shake your hand."

August 10

Angela faced some difficult decisions this week; one involved going to camp. She was to have attended church camp with me, but because of the public way we chose to handle the pregnancy, I offered her the opportunity to go and visit her grandparents instead. "Honey, you've handled this so well, almost too well. Maybe you need a week by yourself, to begin to heal. Why not go to Grandma and Grandpa's?"

I'm not sure what my motives were for suggesting that Angela visit her grandparents. I had been asked to speak each night to the teens. I knew one of the subjects I would have to address would be teenage sexuality. I have always been able to speak honestly and pointedly on the subject of sex, but I didn't know how I would handle this since my family was now compromised. I wondered to myself, *Can I preach with power and authority on this subject now that Angela is pregnant?*

I shared my fears honestly with Angela and warned her that I was under great tension and that she might feel me withdrawing. I also told her that the stress was not the result of her pregnancy, but instead came from doubts about my worth as a father.

"Angela, are you sure you don't want to go visit your grandparents?"

"No, Daddy," she replied quietly. "I have been away from the Lord, and I think I need to go to church camp."

Angela was right. She needed to return to the Lord, and I needed to turn to him with my doubts. Little did we know the blessings that lay ahead.

August 13

Camp was great. It was a time of seeing God fill Angela's bucket! Every day we found time to talk about "the problem," but most of the time she just allowed God and her friends to help her think through all the difficulties she was going to face in the next few months.

Another thing happened at camp. Jim was worried about the pressure Angela and I were under at camp, so Sunday night he called and offered to come. *Oh no!* I thought, *that's all I need — one more pressure to deal with. He'll come and pull his "big man in camp" routine, and that will produce even more pressure.* I told him, "I'm walking a fine line emotionally so if you can come to help and not cause problems then it's okay to come."

Monday night he arrived, and by Tuesday he had made a fool of himself. I explained I was just about over the edge, so for the remainder of the week he shaped up. Not only was he a great help, but he turned out to be a needed friend.

Lord, thank You for using us even when we are empty, or maybe, Lord, You use us especially when we are empty. The healing You created in Angela's heart and the closeness felt between my son and I was needed and a tremendous blessing. Lord, the talk on sexuality was perhaps the best message I've ever given! I want to thank You for Your grace to use us in spite of ourselves. Camp was a blessing.

August 14

When Angela began to suspect that she was pregnant, she told her sister Joani. Joani helped Angela carry the load. She watched her younger sister examine the alternatives and watched her go through periods of guilt, self-justification, doubt, and self-condemnation. She stood by and and tried to carry the load in secret. Joani had even taken Angela to a clinic to verify her pregnancy.

Finally Joani couldn't carry Angela's burden alone, so she told Melissa.

Together, Melissa and Joani finally persuaded Angela to come and tell us.

Now Angela feels betrayed . . . Joani had told Melissa.

Angela is glad the news is out and that she has turned her problem over to God, and she feels good that she has taken the necessary steps to beginning to resolve the situation . . . but she still can't forget that Joani "told" on her.

What do you do? How do you regain trust in someone who for your own best interest "betrays" you?

It's really easy to receive forgiveness, but it's difficult to give forgiveness. Angela is frustrated because her self-doubt returns when she knows she has sinned greatly and gained forgiveness but she is having trouble in giving the same forgiveness to her sister. It's hard to forgive!

Sin is such a terrible enemy. If one sister had not sinned, the other sister would not have had to carry a load she was not mature enough to carry. If one sister had not sinned, we would not be faced with the terrible decision of what to do with the coming baby.

Lord, please help me remember that the one who sins is not my enemy. They are victims of the enemy! Please help my two daughters who were once best of friends to again be close. Lord, help Angela to forgive Joani so she will be able to fully forgive herself. Lord, You have given us many choices. In our case we face the choice of love and forgiveness or bitterness and condemnation. Help us to follow Your example. Fill our hearts with forgiveness.

Matthew 6:14-15 says, "For if you forgive men when they sin against you, your heavenly Father will also forgive you. But if you do not forgive men their sins, your Father will not forgive your sins."

August 16

"Oh Daddy, I wish it were last May . . . if this just hadn't happened! I wish I were ten years old again!" Angela's words have stayed with me all day. My response had been that we can't go back, but because of Jesus, we can start over.

Just the other day I was playing the "If only I had" game. "If only I had not said that." "If only I had not done that." I was playing the "If only I had" game the other day as I was thinking of my oldest two going off to college in just a few days. *What if they're not ready? Has the quality of love and life at our home prepared them for life? What have Bobbi and I done that we could have done differently? How well have we done as parents? Oh Lord, if we could only go back and do things differently!*

At that moment I was looking at them as the children they were, rather than the young adults they have become. I continued thinking . . .

If only I had listened with my heart instead of my ears. If only I had shown more affection. If only I had valued their opinions more openly. If only I had complimented them more often. If only I had taken more time with them individually, prayed more with them than just for them, corrected them with less anger and more grace. If only I had kept my mouth shut when they were distressed and had just been a shoulder for them to lean on. If only I had laughed more with them, thanked them more often for the things they did to please me. If only I had treated them like the treasures they are to me. If only I had learned to enjoy more the things they enjoy doing. If only I had been more forgiving when they failed, trusted them more fully, bragged more about them behind their backs, taken their side above all others, been the first to seek the end of an argument. If only I had spent more time finding out what made them afraid and insecure and sought to remove those things. If only I had remembered to keep my voice quiet and filled with love. If only I had led them more often to the Word of God so they would know more surely that it is there they can find help and direction in times of trouble.

Have you ever played the "If only I had . . ." game?

It is so easy to set yourself up to believe that the success of your child fully depends on how well you do as a parent. "If I fail as a parent, then for sure, my children will fail." Sometimes we forget that if our children are to be saved, then it will be because we have pointed them to Jesus and they have followed our directions to the foot of the Cross. Our children will have to come the same way we did . . . as a sinner, saved by the grace of God!

I can surely identify with Angela, "If only I could go back." But we can't go back, we can only go forward.

We can go to the Father through Jesus the Son and gain His forgiveness for all our past sins! We can go to those we have failed and ask their forgiveness! Then, armed with the grace of God and the time grace provides, we can replace all those old memories of our past failures with brand new memories. And then with the passing of time, we can forgive ourselves.

Lord, help me remember to try to do my best and let You do the rest. Lord, You have said that Angela and I can be brand new in Your forgiveness. Please help me to allow You to do Your healing work in my life. Lord, thank You for being willing and able to do for me the things I cannot do for myself. Thank You for being here.

August 17

As I write today, I'm sorting through the advice of friends — some of it helpful and some of it hurtful. Wisdom is needed to decide what is right for our situation. Again, so many questions.

What shall we do? Angela has fallen in love and has by her sin created a sexual appetite that will cry out for satisfaction. Should we let her continue to see Dan?

The advice seems to fall into two categories: let the kids continue to see each other or separate them. I can still hear the emotion with which each opinion was offered.

"I wouldn't let that boy get within 500 miles of my daughter" one said.

Another said, "Keep that boy away . . . it's all his fault."

Wait a minute. It wasn't rape. Two kids felt emotions they interpreted as genuine love and fell away from the instructions of their parents.

Keep him away? They have only been out three times in their lives. Once they went skating with his family and twice they were selected as prince and princess at a school activity and were escorted by parents. These kids have spent time walking to and from class, talking on the phone. But our kids can't date until they are sixteen.

Keep him away? I'm not sure when they had time to be alone to share sexually!

Yet others say, "Break them up — it's only puppy love. They will get over it."

Another said "Is it really love or just physical attraction?"

My daughter followed her heart instead of her parents' instruction and now we are faced with a problem. Should we let her see him again?

If I say, "You can never see Dan again!" I may discover that her commitment to the boy is greater than her commitment to obey God and her parents.

If I break them up and our daughter goes on to fall in love with another person and marries him, then my daughter, who has become "one" with Dan, will find sexual confusion in her future. When she shares with her husband, her other sexual experience will be there to haunt her and to confuse her. It will hinder her from being able to love her husband fully and completely.

If I let them see each other and they fail sexually again, I will lose my daughter all over again, because to have sex outside of marriage is to lose God's blessing. To lose God's blessing is to separate oneself from God, from one's self, and from one's parents.

I choose to believe my daughter really loves the boy and that she simply chose to love him more than she loves God. My job then is to accept her assessment of love and then to help her learn to love God more than anything or anyone in her life.

Plan of Action:

1. If I have forgiven Angela, then I must forgive Dan too! To say I forgive her with my lips and not forgive him is to assure her that I really have not forgiven her either.

2. I have decided that Angela loves him . . . so must I.

3. Since they have failed physically, I must give them the possibility of becoming husband and wife.

4. It's hard. They will bear a child. But they are too young to drive . . . too young to date . . . too young to marry. Until they mature enough to marry, I must, with his parents' help, provide sheltered times for them to be together to develop what they feel into mature love. This sheltered dating will

provide the time needed for them to earn trust in themselves and trust from their parents.

5. If the boy is to become my son-in-law at some later date, then I must work with his parents so that on the day of their marriage, his parents will receive a daughter they love and trust, and my wife and I will receive not just a son-in-law, but a son-in-heart.

6. To gain God's blessing, they must return to a standard of purity until they marry.

7. If they decide to end their friendship (and the percentages suggest they will), I need to help them end it as friends and part with dignity.

Lord help me! I really do care for Dan. Help me to learn to love him and help his parents learn to love Angela. Help me to know just how much freedom and trust to give. Please help me to treat them like You treat me after You have forgiven me. Lord, please use me to love.

August 19

The time I've dreaded is now pressing upon me. We have to visit Dan and his parents and talk about what to do with the coming baby.

How do you know the will of God? What am I supposed to do as the parent of a fourteen-year-old girl expecting a child?

Angela and Dan rejected God's best . . . and we are now trying to find out what is second best!

Here are the options:

1. ABORTION. Our faith and conviction that life begins at conception eliminates abortion as a possibility. Others may be able to live with this alternative, but Angela rejected this possibility before she told us she was pregnant.

2. MARRIAGE. I believe they are old enough to bear a child, but not mature enough to parent it. I believe their love is of the quality that could lead to marriage, but it is not strong enough at this time to bear the difficulties of that marriage. If they marry at fourteen and fifteen, the divorce rate is nearly 98 percent.

If they marry and move into one of their parents' homes, the pressure of the living situation will never allow the boy to become the head of his own family or the girl to become the wife and mother that God intended her to be.

3. ANGELA KEEPS THE CHILD. If Angela keeps her baby with the hope that she and Dan will be married when they are mature enough, I foresee the following difficulties:

The baby, for the next three to five years, will be raised with its mother as its sister and its grandmother as its mother.

Then, if Angela and Dan marry when they are mature, the baby will be wrenched from the person he (or she) has made an emotional "mother" attachment to.

In trying to be a single parent the baby could find itself "in the way," "inconvenient," "restricting the mother's activities," causing much damage to the child.

If Angela marries someone other than the baby's father, the child may become "yours" in the new marriage and not "ours." The child then compounds the difficulties of that new marriage, also damaging the child.

4. GRANDPARENTS RAISE THE CHILD. Bobbi and I could keep the child and raise it as our own. This option has the most appeal to my selfish nature, but it presents the following problems:

The child will grow up with confusion because its parents are really its grandparents and its sister is really its mom. This may cause the child to question its identity and whether it was really wanted.

If Bobbi and I keep the child, I would be sixty-three when the child graduates from high school. In all honesty, would I be able to meet the child's needs at this age?

In my twenty-three years of ministry I have seen few emotionally healthy children raised by grandparents. Often they are either spoiled or very insecure because of the indulgence or strictness of the grandparents. Would we be any different?

5. ADOPTION. We could find a couple who wants to adopt the child. This alternative also presents problems:

Our daughter would always wonder what was happening to her child. Every child of the same age and sex as hers would make her remember and wonder. "Is that my child? What is my child doing? Is my child all right?"

The child would always wonder why it was with adoptive parents rather than its birth parents.

What then is the "right" answer? What is the will of God?

Since Angela and Dan have sinned, God's best has been removed. Our difficult task then is to find out what is second best.

Facing this decision I find myself filled with many emotions. As I review the five options, I'm filled with anger. None of the alternatives meet everyone's needs.

Kill a child? Let children marry with almost a 100 percent chance of divorce in their future? Let my daughter keep the child and make the child an almost certain point of controversy and conflict? Keep the child ourselves and place the child in a situation where I might be broken of health or mind or even dead when it needs its parents the most? The thought of giving the child up for adoption and never being able to hold it, to spoil it, to teach it about Jesus? I was going to be a great grandparent . . . it's unfair!

Lord, in this moment I feel panic, confusion, and fear. I know that no matter which alternative my daughter and Dan choose, I will lose friends, because it won't be the alternative they would have chosen. Help me to know what is best from Your point of view, so I can guide the kids to the second best decision. Help me to be loving and considerate towards those who hurt me rather than hurt with me. Be with Angela and Dan as they decide, so they will be able to find a way to live with their decision. Please be with the baby. I'm sure glad You are there, Lord. I'm really frightened and empty today. Please help Dan and his parents understand how much we need them right now.

August 21

Today our only son and eldest daughter leave for college. We have mixed emotions. It's difficult under the best of circumstances, but our present crisis only makes it more difficult. Today we say goodbye to Jim and Melissa. There is more on my emotional plate than I can handle.

We loved them into life, watched them learn to walk and talk. We laughed and cried with them, and one by one we watched them accept Jesus as their personal savior.

We watched them being stretched by the teenage years, and now it's time for two of them to leave.

I can remember pressures in the past that made me long for this day to arrive so that Bobbi and I could have fewer pressures and more time to spend together.

The "soon" has come . . . and I'm not ready.

Hidden beneath the hope that soon they would be gone was a much more important hope . . . the hope that our family would truly be a team, united and one. During the last few weeks, the crisis over Angela has been the avenue God has used to answer my prayer. We have been united . . . one! By our joining together to assist Angela, we have been able to lean on the Lord and each other. I've longed for the time when we could be companions . . . a time when we could face the difficulties side by side, rather than from opposite ends of a loud discussion. I've longed for the time when my children could be my friends, and now they are leaving.

Lord, I know they are ready. You have helped them learn to walk and talk, to succeed and fail. You have helped them to establish their own faith and values. They are ready. Look out, world, here they come! Two dynamic young adults who are ready to find their purpose for living, and their mate for loving. Lord, they are ready . . . but I am not.

Suddenly I feel weak, frightened and alone. I know they came into the world one at a time, and they will leave our home one at a time. I know there are still three more in our home to share my life with . . . to fight with . . . to love. But Lord, I will miss the two who are leaving.

Lord, I am so comforted to know that You can be with all those You love at the same time. In moments when I am frightened, please help me take comfort in the fact that You love them even more than I do. Thank You for going with them . . . and, Lord, please help them remember that there is always a place in my heart for them.

August 22

This pregnancy has me questioning myself . . . and I'm not the only one. I woke up this morning to find a letter from Joani:

Dad:

I know you are trying harder to be a better father, but sometimes it's really difficult to understand. I am trying to be the best I can because I feel that if I make one mistake everything you have worked for will go down the drain. But I don't think that the girls *and I can go through the rest of our years at home feeling that you don't trust us. I understand the church and the people are looking at what we do, but if we act like Christians when we go out, why does it matter how much supervision we have?*

I wonder, did you ever have talks with Melissa about how she acted when she was away from home? I never heard one if there was. Is it that you trusted her more than me, or are you worried about me? I think you are worried and you are not sure what I do or how I act around other people. You are not sure because I don't sit down and explain myself and how I feel to you. Well, I am now! I don't drink and I'm still a virgin. I'm not planning on doing anything. I have very strong morals on both subjects because I have seen too many people hurt themselves, their families, and God. I want you to trust me again and not worry about me.

Have I overreacted? Bobbi and I have committed ourselves to the raising of confident, radiant Christians, and to do that we have committed ourselves to trusting the kids until they prove they can't be trusted. Have we allowed the failure of one child to cause us to overreact to the others? How much trust should we give? How much should we react to what others think? Should we care that some are watching us to try to figure out why one child failed? Have I overreacted and caused unnecessary restrictions?

I know that since the pregnancy I have reevaluated everything I do as a father. I've stayed awake night after night trying to see if there are holes I should fill, things I should change, so that my children can be kept from the pain of sin.

Have I tried too hard these last three weeks? Have I forgotten to laugh? I've taken the kids into my room one at a time and tried to show them individual attention so that Angela is not getting all the attention. Has the hurt I've felt and the concern to find godly solutions been all that I've shared with them?

Joani's letter continued:

Please understand that I just feel like you condemn me when you look at me. I don't know if I'm paranoid or what. I just feel like I've done something, when I haven't. I just feel like you won't let me do very much because you think people will talk. I love our church and the people, but I'd just as soon they would let you decide what's good for your family.

You've been a perfect father as far as I'm concerned, and I've always loved you because you trust me, and for some reason, now I feel that you don't.

Oh, I need God's help. I don't ever want to change from being a trusting person. I want to know the balance between loving protection and fearful suspicion. I know if I "give them the name they will play the game." If I give them trust, they will do their best to live up to the trust.

Lord, I need you. Help me to regain balance. Help me so I'm not so frightened about being a father or of the principles we've raised the kids on. Help me restore to all the kids the trust I've always had. My own fears about my fatherhood have imprisoned us all. Please help my children to understand that my new doubts and fears are not produced by their actions, but my own self-doubts as to whether or not I've been a good dad. Please help the kids to be patient with me while You, Lord, are bringing healing to my heart. Father, thank You for Joani who took a risk and opened her heart to write me.

August 23

I'm relieved . . . the session with Dan and his parents went well. We all had come together with many emotions and questions. There seemed to be a mutual concern for the kids. Even though we all agreed that adoption was the best alternative for the baby, we decided that Angela and Dan needed to make the final decision. Dan's parents did not want to know the adoptive parents, so they asked me to contact a minister friend to represent us and begin the search for that special family, using the following criteria:

1. They must be a Christian family.
2. They must have a stable family.
3. They must have good references.
4. They must not know either of our families.

I have conflicting emotions, as I'm sure Angela has. Right now, ten weeks pregnant, she wants to give the baby up for adoption. But how will she feel as the baby begins to grow and she feels life in her womb? I think she will make and remake this decision a thousand times over in the next seven months. How can I help a fourteen-year-old girl and a fifteen-year-old boy find the wisdom and maturity to make such a decision and not waver? Lord, I need Your wisdom.

As I think back over my years in the ministry, I think of different ones who faced this same crisis. Maybe it would help Angela if they wrote to her and shared their experiences. Some, I knew, had opted for abortion; others had kept their child or the child had been raised by the grandparents. A few had married. It might be good to even hear from a boy who fathered a child out of marriage. This will be a job, but I am determined. We need to find an attorney who can inform us of the state adoption laws. We also need financial advice and possible counseling for one or all of us. Again, I find myself feeling overwhelmed. Lord, I need Your strength.

Lord, thanks for Angela. One of the things that is helping me get through this is the fact that she is repentant and tender towards You. If she had been rebellious, I can only imagine the pain I would be feeling. Remind me to tell her that I love her and am proud of her.

31

August 31

It was good to get away for a few days. I had been asked to speak at a Family Camp in California. Driving to and from Family Camp provided time alone to think. The last month has been so intense that moments alone have been rare.

I had time to watch my best friend and his little grand-daughter . . . the way she lights up when her grandpa picks her up. Watching their interaction makes me feel empty.

Oh Lord, give me grace to fill my void. I'm empty of heart and full of tears. Yes, I needed this time away to really face my emotions, to allow myself to feel, to acknowledge my hurt and my emptiness. I needed to see my friend, to confront my loss and then determine to go on.

Lord, a small grain of sand in the soft belly of an oyster turns into a precious pearl. I pray that the small seed of a child will soon turn hurt, embarrassment, guilt, and failure into a precious gift of grace.

September

September 10

Summer is gone and we are experiencing an explosion of activities. Angela is attending school in the day and taking volleyball statistics at night. She has only gained three pounds and there have not been many physical changes yet, so she has chosen to go into hiding, to pretend this isn't happening.

I think she is able for small moments of each day to convince herself it just isn't so . . . "I'm not really pregnant." The one thing that repeatedly makes her face the truth is her inability to keep food down.

Her friends, for the most part, have been supportive and caring. Just yesterday she said, "It isn't quite as hard as I thought it was going to be."

I'm doing the same thing. I've been able to return to work mentally and keep my mind full of activities and the needs of the church. The pregnancy only comes to my mind once or twice an hour.

One thing I'm learning: If I'll take time in the morning to write my thoughts down, and to pray them up to the Lord, I can leave the burden with Him all day long.

Hiding? No, just catching our breath so we can face the next part of what's coming. Soon the clothes will not fit. Soon it will be difficult to walk to school and to classes. Soon it will be obvious to all concerned that a baby is on the way, and then there will be no way of anyone going into hiding.

Hiding? No, just taking time off to fill our buckets so we can go forward.

I remember times in the Lord's life when He left the needs of the multitudes and fled into the mountains or to the seashore for a few moments of "hiding." The constant reality of the cross made it imperative that He find some time to prepare His heart for the coming days.

Lord, help me to know when to allow Angela to go into her private hiding place — to have moments of peace without pressure — and when to help draw her out to face the realities of her "growing" problem.

Thank You, Lord, that when Angela retreats from her parents and from her friends and family that there is never a place so dark or alone that You are not able to be there to share with her those moments in her hiding place.

September 11 (A birthday letter to Angela)

Angela:

Fifteen years ago your mother announced that you were on the way. Days turned to weeks and weeks to months, and it seemed that you would never get here! The last month passed so slowly until suddenly it was the night of your birth. I remember leaving the older kids with friends and bundling up your mom and rushing to the hospital. We waited and waited for the doctor to get there, but he didn't come. Finally, you were through waiting. The nurse told Mom to hold off delivery until the doctor arrived, but I said to your mom, "It's okay Babe, mothers and God have been having babies for a long time . . . let's you and I deliver this baby!"

And then, there you were. Mom, God, and I delivered you into this world all bright-eyed and funny looking. It's been fun watching you grow. To see you set your heart on being a good student and an athlete. I've watched you grow from a little girl into a lovely teenager with all the pressures and changes that come. At times you put too much emphasis on how you looked and you were too concerned about what others thought. I watched you struggle to keep Christ at the center of your life. I've watched you fail, repentant, and then start to believe in God and in yourself all over again. I've been watching you because I love you.

In the future I'm sure you will look back on your fifteenth year and think it was the worst-best year of your life. It was the year you became a woman and left the little girl behind you. It was the year you discovered that God was not only a Savior for your parents, but that He would also be your Savior. It was a year of finding out who your true friends were, and of finding out that "blood is thicker than water" as your family stood by you during every day of your fifteenth year.

Sis, this year will pass. It will bring to you 365 days with all the sadness and happiness you can handle. It will stretch you to the fullest extent of your maturity and you will discover that you are not wise enough, not strong enough to face all those new days. But please remember, the Lord loves you and He will never leave you nor forsake you.

Your mom and I love you and we are glad that God sent you to us fifteen years ago.

Dad

September 12

The same old conflict between Joani and Angela erupted again. Last night there were enough tears that Bobbi needed a dish towel instead of a Kleenex to dry her eyes.

Joani and Angela moved from cold war to open hostility. We have witnessed periodic skirmishes, surprise attacks, and open warfare . . . and we're supposed to be a "Christian family."

It seems long ago when Joani and Angela were the best of friends. They shared every secret and protected each other from every pressure. The happenings of the last year have brought into their lives competition, jealousy, and now, conflict.

Last night I'd had it. Everyone was yelling, Bobbi was crying, and I was fresh out of wisdom and patience.

It was then and only then that I remembered what I should have remembered in the first place . . . *Bill, why don't you allow the Lord to help you? Why don't you get them together and pray?*

We cried and prayed . . . prayed and cried. It was so good to hear them say "I love you." It was so good to see them embrace.

Lord, forgive me when I fail to remember that You are the one who brings harmony . . . that You are the one who tears down barriers. Help me to remember that You want to bring healing to these two girls who long to be close again.

Lord, thank You for Bobbi. She is such a source of strength and help. What a precious friend she is to me. Please help us to cling together, to provide a climate of love so our children can learn through this crisis that You, Heavenly Father, are the blessed healer of all relationships.

September 13

Yesterday a well-meaning person shared with me that he didn't agree with how I was handling my daughter.

I'm trying so hard. When people don't accept our actions or they disagree with our conclusions, it hurts.

"I know if I were in your situation I would . . ."

As humans we often have the tendency to make comments or to draw quick conclusions about another person's difficulties.

Lord, I'm glad You understand. Thank You for being willing to leave heaven to experience all my grief and pain. I think of Your willingness to be poor so that the poor would know You understand; I think of Your willingness to be born to an unmarried girl so that all those born out of wedlock would know You really do understand; I think of how You were willing to be born a Jew, a sometimes rejected and despised people, so that those who are a racial minority would know that You understand their pain; I think of how You were willing to have Your stated purposes for living rejected and torn apart so that those who have dreamed dreams could know You understand. I think of how You were willing to suffer and die so that people who suffer or die in the prime of life can know that You understand. I'm grateful that You were willing to become what we are so that we can become what You are.

September 18

It's amazing how we can deceive others. Just put on a smile, dress up or play a part, and no one will ever know the emptiness of our hearts or the depression that overwhelms us.

I've noticed that Angela is smiling all day and crying all night. Joani is acting typically sixteen. She is concerned with what to wear . . . "Will I have to work on a game night?" "Does that boy really like me?"

Angela, even though she is a year younger, is worrying about adult things. Her concerns are about the coming baby; whether or not Dan will continue to love her; whether his parents will ever accept her. She is carrying an adult load of worries.

It is so difficult to see the end from the beginning. If Angela had only been able to see what the seed sown would bring at harvest time I believe she would never have entered into sin.

I think of David and Bathsheba, the innocent look turned into immorality; I think of Samson flirting with Delilah . . . I don't believe he looked beyond the moment. It's amazing how Satan makes sin look so good. He paints it up so that we are drawn to it. He uses bright lights and empty promises to convince us that "it will be worth it all." It's just like a painted-on smile, there is more underneath than we can see.

Lord, how many things in life are fooling me? The books I read, the TV or movies I choose to watch? It's so easy to flirt with the world — to see how close we can come to the flame without being burned. It's so easy to have the appearance of righteousness and in our minds wish we could live like the world.

I need a house cleaning. I need to see the end from the beginning, and to count the cost before I enter any activity or mind game that Satan brings my way.

I want to be transparent to all those around me. In fact, Lord, help me to be a TRANSparent, so my children can see right through me to You. Help me today to be real and pure, just like You.

September 24

School has started and Angela seems to be adjusting to the fall routine, but I've been aware of her struggling in the area of forgiveness . . . so I thought a letter might help.

Sis:

I know that you received God's forgiveness and that you feel his help and love, but I can still see confusion in your relationship with others, especially Dan's parents. It seems to be very difficult for you to be around them. I believe you need to complete the process of forgiving and being forgiven. This will free you and be a lesson you will remember the rest of your life.

You need to ask for and receive forgiveness from Dan's parents. Often we try to deal with guilt by ignoring it or hoping it will go away. It's easier to blame others. You could be blaming your mom and me for not doing enough to restrict you, or blaming your peers for making you feel like "everyone's doing it," or you could be saying "It's all Dan's fault." The only problem with blaming others for your actions is that it just doesn't eliminate your own feelings of failure and guilt.

In this little letter I want to help you discover that to ask God to forgive you (as you have done) is to receive his forgiveness. When you became a child of God and received his forgiveness, all your past sins were placed under the blood of our wonderful savior and you were declared "not guilty."

When you and Dan sinned you sinned in three relationships . . . you wronged God, others, and yourself.

You made yourself right with God when you claimed 1 John 1:9 "If we confess our sins, he is faithful and righteous to forgive us our sins and to cleanse us from all unrighteousness."

The problem at the moment is that you are having difficulty forgiving yourself and feeling forgiveness from Dan's parents (and there may be others). You need to complete the process of clearing the wrong with others so that you can truly forgive yourself.

Sis, I guess the thing I'm trying to share with you is this: Keep short accounts with God. Confess each day's sins . . . don't haul yesterday's problems and failures into a new day. Ask God to help you be sensitive to others. If you've wronged someone, make it right . . . ask for forgiveness.

I sure love you. I sure like looking into your eyes and seeing all the way into your heart.

Love,

Dad

September 25

It's been several weeks since I've read to Angela what I've written in my journal.

When I read to her about asking people I've known who have also had a baby outside marriage to write to her, Angela seemed very interested.

"Dad, have any of them written yet?"

"Yes," I said, and handed her the letters we had received.

After reading them she responded, "Daddy, I feel like we have to give the baby up for adoption. I want the baby to be happy like our three cousins." (They have been adopted into our family.) "But Dad, I'm afraid that I'll change my mind after the baby is born and want to keep it. Daddy, I'm afraid I'll change my mind."

"Angela, I've changed my mind every time I've thought about what you should do. One minute I'm thinking of the baby, and I think we should find a family that can't have a child and give them a gift of a baby to love . . . the next minute I'm thinking about you and thinking it would be best for you to keep it . . . the next minute I'm thinking of myself, and I think I'll die if we give the baby away.

"I know that during the next months you will watch your body grow and expand. Soon you will feel the first tiny kick of the baby, and before you know it you'll be ready to deliver a brand new life into this world. I'm sure that many times during the next few months you'll wonder if you made the right decision.

"I've told you that what is best is behind us . . . what is second best is in front of us, and the Lord will have to lead us to it. I want you to know that your mom and I will try to be honest with you all the way. Sometimes we will come to an opinion as to what we think you should do that will differ from your opinion.

"But there is one thing I want you to remember: Your mom and I will support you and your decision. You will probably change your mind a thousand times, and we may become frustrated with you, but please know that with all our hearts we will support what you decide. I don't know what is right, best, and proper. I just know that whatever you decide, you will have to live with the rest of your life.

"One thing has been decided. Mom and I love you and always will."

September 26

Several more letters have come for Angela. It meant so much to me that these dear ones would take the time to share their stories with her. In fact, the whole family has been blessed in reading them. I had asked them to write and share three things: their testimony, their counsel to Angela, and their counsel to Bobbi and me.

From a girl who gave her child up for adoption:

Dear Angela,

Your dad came to me about a month ago and explained your situation to me. First of all, I want you to know that I cried for you because whatever decision you make will be very hard and painful, but remember that God loves us so much even through our mistakes; that's the wonderful thing about God's love. He can take something as horrible and ugly as my sin and turn it into something beautiful and glorifying to him. I must totally let go and let him work.

As you know, I was in that same situation as you and I do know what you are going through. All I want to do is share with you how God brought me through it. I don't want to talk you INTO anything. You and God must make your decision. No one else can, so don't let them . . . TRUST IN GOD.

I was so excited about having a baby. I love kids. I wasn't thinking about anything but the fun, cuddly, cute baby, not the responsibility. I felt this way for eight months. Then someone suggested I give up my baby for adoption. I thought they were crazy and wouldn't even think of it. But God wouldn't let me forget that idea.

The thought of adoption worked on me until I finally was convinced that it was the best thing to do. When I got it down in black and white on paper, I had no doubt in my mind. I had to give her up. I had to think clearly and logically about the baby's welfare. I couldn't give her much, and yet, I wanted her to have everything. I tried to justify keeping her because I wanted to keep her more than anything. But because I loved her I had to give her up. That was tough because I already had baby clothes, blankets, crib, bathtub, etc. I even had her name picked out. All the baby things reminded me over and over about what I was doing, but God was faithful and he gave me peace and assurance that I can't even explain to you. It was so real and so wonderful . . . I knew I was doing the right thing. That didn't mean I didn't do my share of crying and grieving. I did! That's okay though . . . tears are good.

With the help of some very wonderful people, family and friends (a lot of help from your dad), I wrote letters to five couples who were unable to have children. I had made up a questionnaire to find out certain things about those couples. I wasn't going to give my baby to just anyone off the street.

The most important thing I wanted to know about them was their spiritual life. I wanted my baby to know Jesus. Four of these couples wrote back and there were two letters that really touched my heart. But I could only choose one. After I made my decision I felt that same peace and assurance as before. Then about a month later, I got a message that the couple I didn't choose had become pregnant . . . isn't God wonderful?

I hope you can see how beautifully God worked through the situation. There are so many couples — good Christian couples who want babies but can't have them.

I dedicated her to God's hands when I gave her up. I have no regrets in the decision. I do have peace but also curiosity. I'd like to know how she is doing, when she took her first step, what her first word was. And every February fourth I stop and remember her, saying a special prayer for her along with the daily ones.

I will always have a longing for my daughter and I do cry about it sometimes, but God really helps. I hope to have a child of my own some day with the wonderful husband God gave me.

This letter was hard for me to write. I've prayed about it the last month. I hope I haven't offended you or turned you off. I just wanted you to know that you are not alone. People do care and you are not trapped. God can make anything beautiful.

From a girl who kept her baby:

Dear Angela,

Hi! My name is Mary. I'm twenty-six, married, and have two children. My youngest is two and a half, my oldest is eleven. By the age of my oldest son, it's evident I had him when I was very young (fifteen). I understand that you are also in that position.

I'm writing in the hope that what I can tell you might be a source of encouragement to you. I want you to know, first of all, that you are not alone. What's happening to you has also happened to others. Every situation is a little bit different, but we all have the same emotions, the same hurts. Not knowing your particular situation, it's a little hard for me to write, but let me tell you some of what I was feeling.

It was a time of great confusion. I felt like nothing was straight in my head. I didn't know which way to turn, who to face, what to do. It was easier after my family found out — there were some decisions made.

I was scared a lot. There were so many things changing physically, situation-wise, that it was overwhelming. I was afraid of being found out, of what people would say to me and about me. I was afraid of the pain and of being sick. I was afraid of losing what I had so desperately hung onto. I felt guilty because of what had happened, the things I had been involved in. I was also hurt emotionally. My boyfriend left the situation as soon as it was evident I was pregnant. He was still around, school and places where I was, but not with me. That was also hard to deal with emotionally.

I came to the point one evening where I really wished I could die. I didn't want to live through what was ahead. I think the one reason I didn't do anything about it was the baby inside me and the many people who were praying for me. I realized soon after that I needed more, I really needed the God I had shunned for so long. I took a turn around and accepted what the Lord could do for me. After that, everything was not perfect, there were still struggles, I was still pregnant, I still hurt and I still had to deal with the situation, but the difference was I was not all by myself. God was carrying me through all that was ahead.

I can't remember much else. As time goes by, a lot of the hurts will heal and you will find some things hard to remember. I struggled a lot through my high school years and even after that, but time really does have a way of healing. Every year that passes seems to make some memories fade even further. Hearing that now may be impossible to believe . . . I didn't believe it either. But now, twelve years later, I have a better perspective. In some ways the pain never goes away, but it does fade.

I do want to advise you in one thing. When it comes time for your delivery and when you begin to plan for that time, plan on having someone go with you for the WHOLE time — clear through the time the baby is born. My mom left when it was time for delivery and that was the scariest, most alone feeling I ever had.

I know this is long. I'm sorry, I hope not too long. I want you to know I will be praying for you. If you have any questions you want to ask, please write back and ask. I'll do my best at answering. Keep your head up and be proud of who you are. A friend gave me a very special Bible verse when I was struggling. It has been an encouragement to me through the years and I now pass it on to you in hopes that it will give you strength, also.

"I can do all things through Christ who gives me strength" (Philippians 4:13).

The following letter was tucked in with Angela's but was addressed to Bobbi and me.

I would like to encourage you to really think through all your options concerning the coming child. Adoption is great and positive as long as everyone feels strongly in that direction. But the one it's hardest on is the one who is pregnant. It's an easier way for the family and for the daughter, but sometimes easiest is not best. I've heard several people who really regret giving up their first child. From my experience, I feel that it probably would have been easier, but, if I had given him up, it would have been more damaging. Having my son and keeping him gave me a sense of responsibility and accountability that I never would have known otherwise. It would have been easy for me to fall right back into the lifestyle I was living in before I got pregnant. It enables me to say "No, I can't smoke or drink or sleep with you" because I have a responsibility to my son at home.

From a daughter of an unwed mother who now has adopted children:

Dear Angela,

I've tried to write for a number of weeks, but I've found it almost impossible. What should I share? What would be right? What is actually the truth? So many feelings have emerged.

I am a mother with an adopted son. My mother was unwed and only fifteen when I was born.

Let me share about my mom. Her life as an unwed mother was lonely, even with her family near. She wanted to raise me, so she put me into a foster home (private type), went to work for four months and nearly dropped from fatigue. As fall approached, she knew she must finish her education in order to get a job and support me; a ninth grade education was not enough. Her young boyfriend cared, but was so young there was nothing he could do. She told me she just couldn't bear to give me up, so she turned down many offers from couples who wanted to give me a home, family and love. Her dream that someday things would change never came true, so I grew up not having an adopted family or even a natural family. Life was an endless struggle just to survive.

As hard as it would seem, O how I wished she would have loved me just a little more and given me to a couple who would hold, love, and protect me.

I could write pages about the pain of not being part of a whole family. I can't be impartial, my precious mom needed guidance, prayers and forgiveness, but none of that was available.

As a child of love, now an adult, I would encourage you to love enough to let go.

Angela, I don't want to end on that sad note, but instead want you to know that now I am the mother of a beautiful little boy, a boy whose mother gave him to my family when we wanted a child so very much. The joy is beyond description. I'm so thankful to the precious young mother who loved so much she let that little one become ours. We love you and pray for the decision you are facing.

A letter from a girl who had an abortion:

I was talking to your parents the other day, and they said that you are thinking about giving up your baby. I'm glad that you are seeking advice before you make the biggest decision of your life.

I wish that I could have been able to make up my own mind, but my parents said "You are having an abortion!" I didn't want to cause my parents any more heartache than they already had, so I had it done.

What happened to me? I was raped in late fall and was sick and missed my menstrual cycle the next month. I was so sick I went to the doctor and he gave me the pregnancy test and it turned out positive.

Even though I thought I might be pregnant, I was not prepared for the outcome of the doctor's examination. I was scared to death. What am I going to do? Should I keep the baby? I had heard about abortions, and I knew in my heart I just couldn't do it.

When I told my parents, my mother said, "I've been a bad mother . . . Christian girls don't get pregnant!"

Without asking me, Mom called the doctor's office and asked for a doctor in another town who would do an abortion. When I got home from school she told me that I had an appointment.

I was not asked what I wanted to do . . . I was told. At that point I didn't argue, get upset, or leave the house because I loved my parents too much to hurt them more.

My father went with me to the examination and then for the hospital stay. I saw the doctor on Monday and had the abortion Tuesday. My father was very understanding through the whole ordeal. The nurses got me ready. There were four of us to have an abortion that day and I was last. They wheeled me into a little room, put me on the table, and put an IV in my arm so I wouldn't get dehydrated nor lose too much blood. They put some sleeping medicine in the IV tube, and I was half awake. There was just enough medicine so I didn't feel the pain of what the doctor was doing. It took him about forty-five minutes and when he was done he just threw the fetus into a fifty-gallon barrel with the others.

I cried and cried . . . "What have I done? God, please forgive me for this mistake!"

I left the hospital around 4:00 P.M. weak and very empty. I have regretted doing it for years.

I wonder what he or she would be like as big brother or sister to my other children? I know the age and grade in school . . . How would he or she like it, and how would he or she be as a student or a person?

You will probably think about your decision in the years to come. Maybe you will wish you had not gotten pregnant at all. But you can't change the fact that you did.

Remember the times with your parents during these nine months. Try to understand their point of view, but don't let them run your life without talking about all the ways to handle the pregnancy. Talking is the best way to say "I love you very much."

A letter from a minister's daughter who kept her baby and later married the father:

Dear Angela,

I have been meaning to write to you for quite a while, but with four sons underfoot, I can't sit very long. I hope you don't mind me sharing with you my experience. When we were told that you were pregnant, a whole flood of memories and emotions came to me. When I was fifteen, my mother figured out that I must be pregnant. She was hurt that I had had premarital sex. I had to go with my dad to get the test. It was positive. We talked about abortion, but I ruled that out right away. I was scared to death.

I can remember lying alone in my room in agony, crying to God that I would wake up from my nightmare. I felt so alone. Nobody could really share my feelings. The boy was sixteen; he wasn't too upset. I think he liked the idea.

I was really confused. I didn't know what to expect. I guess the shame and guilt was the worst. My parents took over pretty much. My dad was a minister, so we had to tell the church. In the end, everyone was very loving and accepted me. That really helped.

There was the question as to whether to give the baby up or keep it. EVERYONE had the answer. All were different. It was left up to me. I heard of so many couples who wanted my baby, and I felt guilty to not let them adopt it. But I knew in my heart that I couldn't give my baby away. I have always wanted to be a mother anyway.

I grew up fast that year. My friends didn't really understand, although I had a few stick with me. I went back to high school until I was eight months along. I was quite an attraction. "The preacher's daughter is pregnant!"

At the beginning of my eighth month I went to a young mother's school. Some gave up their babies and some of us kept ours; we each respected the other person's decision. It helped to be in a situation where girls were in the same condition as I.

My mom was my birth coach. My dad was with me in the labor room too. It was work, but when my son was born, we all knew he was our special gift. I lived at home until my son was two and a half years old, and then I graduated from high school. Mom babysat my son or I took him to school with me. My boyfriend and I had a lot of growing up to do. We dated other people. We acted like typical teens, but we were proud of our son even though I didn't really know how to fully care for him.

We got married when we were only eighteen. Those were hard years. Growing up is difficult enough, but with a baby even more so.

Here I am at twenty-seven, finally traveling the road that God wants me to. Each of my sons is special and loved, but I think that my first son will always be a favorite to my family, he was the first.

I sure don't envy you and the decisions you have to make. Seek advice, but only you know what is right in your heart.

We love you . . . call any time you want to chat.

September 30

It's been a good week. There were the normal tensions in the family and at church, but it's been a good week.

Yesterday was my "day off" and I spent the morning at a Christian Education conference and ministered at a funeral in the afternoon. Late afternoon I took a much-needed nap. When I woke up, the kids were in a great mood and so we played games for an hour and laughed and teased. It seemed like the pressure and tension of the week just faded away.

Now it's Sunday morning and it's amazing how prepared I feel for all the busy activities of the day. Proper rest and time with the family all add up to a more relaxed minister . . . ready for all a Sunday brings.

Lord, thank You for the rest that comes in prayer, naps, and laughter. Will You please ease the pressure of each one of Your flock who worships here today. Make the Bible school and worship hour a refreshment to a weary flock. May they leave renewed in spirit and prepared for the coming week. Help me to see the needs and to reach out to those who need that special touch of Yourself this day. Thank You, Lord, for filling my life with joy.

October

October 1

I'm so glad I'm in the ministry! During the past twenty-three years I have watched people react in crisis in many different ways . . . some of them illustrated the love of Christ and some of them did not.

Have you ever been in a room without doors? Or at least it seemed like the situation provided no escape?

Had I not been in the ministry, involved in others' lives when the going was rough, I might not have been able to support Angela in her time of need.

I learned a lesson many years ago that I have never forgotten.

It was around noon when the phone rang and a frightened woman asked me to come to her home. She was crying so much I didn't know what had happened, and so I went in much fear. When I arrived, I discovered a terrified mother of a fourteen-year-old girl named Mary. When I arrived at her home, Mary was in her bedroom with her older brother, and the mother struggled to tell me that her daughter was three months pregnant by a fifteen-year-old boy. She said her husband was on the way home from work and that she was afraid he would throw his daughter out of the home.

When the father arrived, he noticed the oldest son's car, my car, and was sure something terrible had happened. When he burst through the door his wife threw herself into his arms and sobbed out her story, "Mary is pregnant!"

What did the father do? Rather than thinking of himself, his first thought was of his daughter and her welfare. "Where is Mary?" he asked. "Is she all right?"

His first response? Not one of a man caught in a room without doors, a situation without any alternatives. In that split second he had chosen to act like the Lord Jesus.

He called for Mary to come into the room and took that very immature little girl onto his lap. Here are some of the things he said that afternoon:

"Mary, I don't think any less of you this afternoon than I did when I left for work this morning." Pointing out the window, he said, "See that mountain? A mountain is only really large the first time you see it. Start climbing it and it gets smaller every day . . . you and I are going to climb that mountain one step at a time. Mary, we are a close family, and we'll make it together."

Angela, I'm so glad to be a minister. I've had the wonderful opportunity to watch God work through a frightened father to bring grace to a guilty daughter. I'm so glad that I could learn from watching so when you said, "Daddy, I'm pregnant," I knew God could work through me to help you.

Angela, sometimes it seems that we have no alternatives, but with God in our lives we are never in a room without doors. The Lord Jesus said He would never leave you nor forsake you. Keep looking up!

October 13

As I watch Angela endure the consequences of her sin, I'm forced to realize how much of what we do affects those around us.

When Dan is kind, encouraging or thoughtful, she is filled with happiness. When he forgets to call, fails to notice her appearance, or is negative or unkind, her poor human heart is broken, and all the pieces of her puzzle are thrown into an uproar.

Lord, I'm thinking today of the many times I've been harsh or thoughtless to my dear wife and family. Thanks for revealing to me how my actions affect those around me, especially my family.

I need to be more like You, Lord, so that the influence of my life upon others will be one of help and not hurt, encouragement and not discouragement. I need to reflect the principles in 1 Corinthians 13 — patient . . . kind . . . not jealous . . . not bragging or arrogant, rude or indecent . . . not acting poorly or seeking things only for myself . . . not easily upset or remembering those things others have done to me that I said I'd forgiven.

Help me to rejoice with good things and not justify my own sin and failure by being glad about the failure of those around me. Help me to bear up under all that comes my way . . . to believe in those in my world . . . to always be hopeful in every circumstance and to endure whatever others place upon me. Help my love to be such that it outlasts anything those around me might do to me, so that when my life is over they will remember me for my love and Christlike spirit.

Give me patience when people fail me or let me down. When I feel drained by their actions, words, or attitudes, help me remember that Your love for me is such that You will be there to produce joy in my heart — not just happiness that depends on circumstances, but the inner joy of the Holy Spirit that allows me to rise above the circumstances, the disappointments of life.

Lord, thank You that we are not depending on ourselves or upon Dan to meet Angela's needs. Her joy is not dependent on whether or not she is homecoming princess, a yell leader, or whether she can get into her clothes or not. I thank You, God, that we just have to depend on You for our needs during this critical time.

October 21

Dear Angela,

Sometimes it's easier to share my thoughts with you in writing, especially if it's something I want you to think about for a while. I sense you've been doing some serious thinking lately. As your father, I want to share some observations I've made about you. I feel I need to confront and challenge you, but as always, in love.

I've watched your purpose for living vary, depending on whatever objective you had your eyes on at the moment. I've watched you try to be an athlete . . . to be popular . . . to get good grades . . . to find a best friend . . . to find a special friend to love.

I've watched you search for an answer to the universal question, just why am I alive?

I've seen you sometimes drift without a purpose and become bored, frustrated, or angry. I've watched you select "second-class objectives" and when you accomplished what you set out to do you wonder, Is that all there is?

Forgive me if I sound like I'm preaching . . . I'm trying very hard not to. I only want you to know we all struggle with this question at times in our lives; I guess it is part of being human.

I know you remember that you were "created in the image of God." I know that you accepted Jesus as your Savior. I know there have been moments in your life when you not only allowed Jesus to be your Savior, but to be your Lord. Those were happy times. You spent time praying and reading your Bible. Your love for God was evident by your obedience to Him. I know those times were precious to you. But Angela . . . what about now? What is happening now? What does the Lord want of you? Let's stop and think of now even though it may be difficult.

I wonder if some of the following questions are going through your mind these days?
 Am I here just to please my parents?
 Will someone ever want to marry me?
 Will I ever be a parent someday?
 Will my peers ever honor me for something good I've done?
 Will I ever contribute something significant to humanity?
 Can God ever use me for His glory?

Angela, you are here to demonstrate what God can do through a person who accepts him. People are looking at you, yes, even now in this difficult time they are watching you, looking to see the Lord Jesus in your life. Maybe at times you cannot see or feel His presence, but He is there just the same.

Sis, you are alive so people will see your good works and glorify your Father who is in heaven! You are alive so you can allow the Lord Jesus to purify and beautify your life in such a way that people will be able to look right past you to see God. They will see that if God can do that for you, then He can do the same thing for them!

There are still marks in my life that keep you and others from seeing Christ in my life. Sometimes I'm thoughtless, sometimes I'm moody or angry. Sometimes the marks in my life take the form of wrong thoughts or hasty actions, but since I accepted Christ He has been living in my life to build me into His image (Ephesians 2:8–10).

Please pray for me and I'll pray for you that we will be able to remove any sin or blemish that detracts from the One who lives within each of us.

I love you . . . nothing makes me prouder than the times when I can see Jesus shining out of your life. He is the purpose for living.

November

November 11

For the last few weeks I've been hiding from the coming baby. Other concerns have taken my thoughts and energy, and even though it seems like every other TV program is about a girl who gave up her baby, I've been hiding.

Several days ago Angela said, "Mom, what does a baby's kick feel like?" She felt the flutter in her stomach, the proof of life within her. She no longer can ignore the coming baby by wearing oversized clothes . . . no longer pretend that she is not pregnant. The baby is now announcing its presence and will do so until it is ushered into the world.

I continue to praise the Lord for Dan. His phone calls, his tenderness, his teasing, and yes, even his abrupt anger at times is just what Angela needs. I never will forget his contribution to her well-being.

Soon we parents will meet with Dan and Angela to read the letters of application for the baby. I am having trouble with this. It is tempting to stay busy, to push the thoughts about the coming baby out of my mind. This isn't good and it can't go on.

I know that Angela and Dan have been confident from the beginning that they want to give the baby up for adoption, but the closer it gets the more difficult it becomes. Am I being selfish? Am I just thinking about my grandchild being away from my love and care? My head tells me that it's best for the baby to go into a home that is emotionally and spiritually prepared to parent the child, but my heart cries "No!"

Lately I've found myself thinking about the other alternatives for the coming child. I've thought about the kids getting married, or having Angela keep the child, or us keeping the child. I must guard my heart and stick with the decision that is best for the baby, that is, to have a home that is capable of meeting its every need.

Lord, I know that if I'm having these thoughts Dan's parents must be having second thoughts too. Please help me to be in charge of my feelings so I can be objective in this decision. Thank You, Lord, for Dan. He's such a fine boy. Please help all of us to find just the right family to raise and love the child so it will love You too. Thank You, Lord, for being here.

November 15

Yesterday I returned home from a speaking engagement in California. It was great to join the family at Jim's wrestling event. I couldn't help but marvel at the growth in my son. A real peace is evident in his life, and he welcomes me with warm affection. It was only a few years ago that we could hardly be in the same room without tension, but we made it through those difficult days.

Looking back, I can thank God for those days, for in them God stretched my faith. His faithfulness is constant and His Word is true. Someone has said that the best definition of faith is trusting in the integrity of God. God will always be there. He won't allow anything to come upon us that we cannot carry with His help. God's faithfulness in the past has made it easier to trust Him with the present. Thank You, Lord, for times of stretching.

November 29

I'm so weary, Lord . . . this present crisis is affecting my sleep, my sex life, even my ability to concentrate. I'm not preaching great sermons, so Lord, help me to **be** *a great sermon.*

Lord, thank You for my home. It's a good place to be. Thank You for being with my family in my absence, for Your protection the week when the temperature dropped to zero among other things! Yes, this was the week the furnace quit for two days. This was the week of heavy snow and Bobbi slid off the road twice in one short evening. Melissa wrecked the truck and the flu bug decided to attack. This week was a nightmare but the family survived. Thank You for Your faithfulness, forgive me for so often taking that for granted.

Lord, today is Thanksgiving Sunday. I pray that everyone who enters church today will feel Your presence. May they know by faith that You are really God and that You care so much.

Thank You for the presents You sent me this year. Some of them have been wrapped in very ugly paper, but Lord, once I've unwrapped them the Scriptures proved true that "every good and perfect gift" comes from You.

December

December 5

Why is it that as we grow older we often lose the ability to laugh?

As a young boy I discovered the gift of laughter and was delighted when I found I could make others laugh.

When I entered college and abruptly faced the realities of adult life, I somehow lost that precious gift. It wasn't until I met my friend, Fred, that I discovered that as an adult you could be both serious and crazy.

I watched Fred use that wonderful humor to love and direct a church, and I watched the church love him and follow him to the glory of God. I also watched Fred lose his sense of humor. I thought at the time, *I'm never going to lose my sense of humor; there will always be something to laugh at.*

A few years ago the tension in our home built to the breaking point. I had to either change or crack — I cracked. The next two years crushed me, and a war developed between my son and me — a war that stripped me of every smile, every giggle, every laugh.

He was not really doing anything terrible; he was just trying to grow up and I was having a hard time letting him.

Look at me now, in the midst of much greater problems I'm standing tall (as tall as a short man can stand), smiling and even discovering that I can laugh and be silly.

Lord, thank You for times of tears that remind us of how frail and delicate we are. Thank You for the gift of laughter so that we can see beyond the defeats, beyond the failures, to laugh at ourselves and discover the great and wonderful balance of a faith that works itself out through laughter.

Lord, I know that in the months ahead I might take the situation too seriously. Please help me to smile, because nothing, NOTHING can defeat me if You, Lord, are in my life.

December 16

The anxious days of selecting a family for the baby are finally in the past. We now have a wonderful couple who will adopt the baby. This was an enormous decision and it is with great relief that the choice is made and we are all in agreement. As I look back, I can see God's guidance in all the many details. We thank Him for the way He fit the pieces together and gave us just what we needed to make the right choices.

Angela and Dan decided it would be best to give the baby up for adoption. I contacted a minister friend and asked him to be our "go-between" with the prospective parents.

We all agreed it would be best for the baby if it could grow up with its own family — parents, aunts and uncles, grandparents. So we decided we should not know where the baby was, but that we would send the adoptive parents a packet of pictures and facts that would allow the baby to find us if the adoptive parents deemed it necessary for the child's well-being.

When a prospective family called our minister friend, they were asked to send their application, family description, pictures, and a written statement of why they wanted the baby. Our friends then removed all identifying items and delivered the information to us. We then carefully went through the information and eliminated any potential risks before turning over the information to Angela and Dan for their approval or disapproval. It was the conviction of all four parents that the kids had created the problem, and only if they made the final decision would they be able to live with it.

Sunday night and the following next few days the kids pored over many letters. What an emotional time as just the right family was sought. All the families were acceptable. All were wanting a baby, but this was "our" baby and how very much we wanted God's choice.

Dan and Angela finally made a choice. The next day our go-between called the couple and asked:

"Do you still want the child?"

"Are you able to qualify according to state law?"

"Are you able to care for the financial responsibilities including pre- and post-natal care, hospital, lawyer and court costs?"

The family joyfully said yes to all the questions and the pressure began to lessen in our home.

Our minister friend called my office and with tears shared how thrilled the couple were about being selected. He called an hour later and said he had talked to them again, and they were still weeping with joy.

As a man who will never be able to hold his first grand-child, never be able to spoil it or watch it receive Christ, the news of how very much the child was wanted brought healing to my troubled heart.

The next day I had the joy of hearing my daughter say, "Dad, I feel so much better knowing how much they want my baby."

As we approach the Christmas holidays, I am comforted by the joy we are giving the couple who couldn't have a baby. Picturing their joy in my mind helps me accept the coming loss.

Lord, You have not left us alone one second. Your grace, Your love has surrounded us every step along the way. Thank You that You have allowed me to experience what You can do with failure in my own life, and now I'm watching You care for my daughter in spite of her failures. It helps me to know that when, not if, she and the other children fail in some way, You will be there to help them though their difficulties. Thank You that some young couple will have a special Christmas this year.

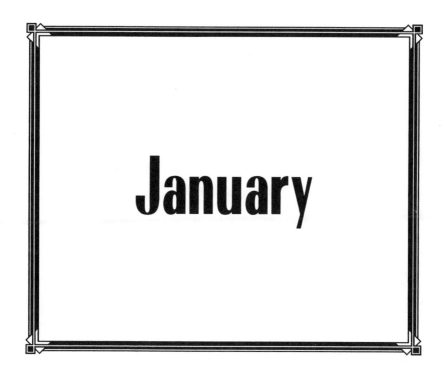

January

January 4

Christmas was wonderful. Something very special happened this year. My brothers, sister, and their families gathered at my parents' house and God used this family gathering to speak to all of us.

After all the fun of opening the packages and taking pictures, while the wrappings were still on the floor, my sister-in-law brought a special "package" into the room and hand delivered it to my brother. I thought it was a puppy, but when he looked in the box, he found his newly adopted daughter with a special envelope pinned to her dress.

Months ago, my brother and sister-in-law drove back east to pick up a little girl they were adopting. The previous months had been filled with one problem after another delaying the final adoption. Then, on the day before Christmas, the letter from the court arrived . . . she was officially theirs. And now, here she was, in the middle of the wrapping paper with the letter officially making her theirs pinned to her dress.

What a joy it was to watch happiness flood my brother's face. Bobbi and I brushed away a tear, and in my heart I thanked God for the fact that He had used the technicalities . . . the legal system . . . the mail so that Angela and the rest of the family could be there to see the rejoicing over a little adopted girl.

Lord, thank You for the baby of Bethlehem who became our Savior and made it possible for us to find peace in a very troubled time. I love You, God.

January 16

It is early Sunday morning. My heart is broken. In twenty some years of preaching I have watched the Lord bring healing to family after family. Not one family who was intimately a part of the church has divorced — they have always reconciled. But during the last few months while I've been concentrating on my daughter, I've been watching three families split up and face divorce.

One troubled woman, who last year divorced her husband, married another, and had that marriage annulled, is now wanting to return to her first husband. Lord . . . how can I help her?

Another is a mature couple who have already endured the tragedy of divorce in their past, and even though they became Christians fifteen years ago, they want to separate. One is threatening suicide and the other has withdrawn from reality. I sent them to a counselor, but even this is not working. It's causing great concern in the church.

The third burden is a young woman of only twenty-four. She is married to a fine Christian, but she left her husband and family and is now pregnant with the child of another man.

Lord, today is Sunday. My sermon is on paper, my heart is empty. Unless you take the sermon and through me make it meaningful to those who come, it will stay on the pulpit instead of filling hungry hearts. Please take my troubled heart and use me. I'm so empty, so filled with self-doubt. Grant me grace and peace so I can give it away to those who come to worship today. Lord, thank You for being here. I need You so.

January 20

Things at home are fine. Those troubled marriages in the church are not.

During this time when other people's problems seem more intense than mine, the weeks have just flown by.

Angela is continuing to be a blessing as she develops her servant's heart. She, who was once so selfish that she was difficult to be around, is now the first one to see a need and try to meet it. She is busy cooking and cleaning, and is the first one to help her mother or give up something of hers to help someone else. What a change.

I thought for a while that she was somehow trying to "repay" God or her parents for what she has done . . . but the joy she shows, the love that radiates from her while she is serving is not payment, it's transformation!

Yesterday I picked her up from school and took her to the doctor. Those hours together were really fun.

Lord, I'm so grateful for Your Word that says "God causes all things to work together for good to those who love God, to those who are called according to His purpose"

"Daddy, I'm Pregnant!"

(Romans 8:28). I'm so grateful for Your Word that doesn't say that all things are good. Lord, the fact that my daughter sinned is not good — there are scars. But Lord, the way You are taking what was bad and turning it into something good is wonderful. Thank You for a little girl who failed, sought Your face and found it, and is now becoming a radiant Christian servant. Your Word is true!

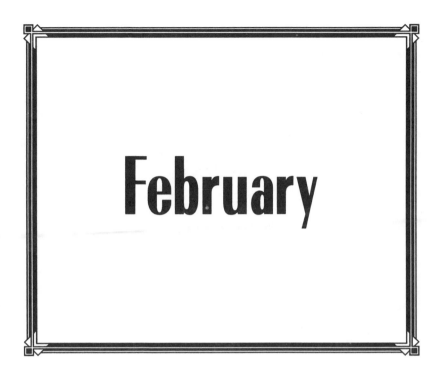

February

February 8

Bobbi and I just returned from a much-needed vacation. I appreciate so much that this is encouraged by the church. The kids enjoyed having one of our church families stay for the week. This gave us all a brief change of pace from the constant pressure we've been under.

You can't run away from problems. Even though we fled for a week from the pressures of a pregnant daughter and three failing marriages at church, they were here waiting for us when we returned.

As I look at sin and the way it reaches out to every relationship in our lives, I sometimes feel overwhelmed by its utter devastation. The phone is ringing off the hook from so many hurting people.

If I keep my eyes on You and I stay a man of faith, then I will be a source of encouragement to those in my world. If I fall apart by keeping my eyes on the difficulties in my own home or in my own world, then my failure will hurt those I love most. Please help my trembling heart to become calm. Please help me to keep my heart set on heaven and my eyes on the possibilities rather than the difficulties.

Lord, I'm more frightened today than I've been for some time.

February 11

"Daddy, I'm afraid!"

"What about, Angela?"

"I'm afraid about how much it will hurt when the baby is born."

Angela has been listening to other women recounting vivid tales of the pain and trauma associated with the birth of their children. As a man I have never been able to figure out why women like to tell the painful aspects of childbirth and why some women hardly remember the pain.

What joy Bobbi and I shared with the birth of our five children. I remember the "count-down" as we timed the pains, the water breaking at home, the rush to the hospital and then the excitement we experienced in welcoming our children into the world.

The pain? I love Bobbi for the price she has paid in giving life to the children. A dad's pain? It was real. I remember the fingernail scratches up and down my arms, the weariness of my mind and body as I waited with Bobbi through the difficult hours, the relief of the announcement "It's a boy" or "It's a girl." I remember checking very carefully the fingers and toes to see if all the parts were there. I remember the thrill of naming our child and the joy of calling our families "collect" to let them know we had received an addition to our family.

I remember silly things. I remember having a banner to welcome Jim home and having a tiny football as a gift for him. I remember arriving at the hospital just eleven minutes before the birth of Melissa. I remember waking up Bobbi to tell her Joani was coming and, because of the medication, waking her up to tell her the baby was here. I remember the doctor not arriving on time for Angela's birth and the nurse not knowing what to do, so I said, "Come on, Babe . . . God and mothers have been having babies for a long time . . . let's go ahead and have this baby." I remember Melody being born at 9:43 on Sunday morning, and I was able to get back to the church to preach the sermon on "the new birth." Oh yes, I remember the kids wanted to name her "Breakfast."

I remember many happy things about having babies — little pain but many wonderful memories. It's hard this time. Our daughter will have the baby for only minutes, and the adoptive parents will have the child for a lifetime.

I'm not so afraid of the stretching of the body, the pains of birth, the final squeeze and then the entrance of a baby into the world as I'm afraid of the pain of stretching our minds and lives to anticipate a child and then experiencing the vacuum the child will leave as it fills the void of some other family.

The pain? Oh it's real.

I too am afraid . . . but not of the physical pain. I'm afraid of emotional pain that only God can heal. I'm worried that I'll break down and not be strong when I must be strong. The decision is already made, the baby will be going to a family who will love it as a "gift of God." I must be strong and allow the Lord to comfort my heart so I can reinforce Angela and Dan's decision.

Lord, I'm in pain. I'm not coping very well. Angela will start childbirth classes tomorrow. Giver her maturity beyond her years and grant her Your comfort.

February 15

Some weeks ago, my friends encouraged me to mail some of what I had written to Dr. James Dobson of *Focus on the Family*.

I had felt frustrated by not being able to find any help in print for Christian fathers when a daughter is pregnant.

Dr. Dobson's organization called yesterday to confirm that they want me to come to southern California and participate in a radio broadcast on the subject.

Lord, I don't know how You want this experience to be used. I believe that some of the things I've written to You and my daughter might help others. Please help me know what to share and what not to share.

I've asked Angela and Dan for their permission to mail a section of my journal called "My Missing Daughter Has Come Home" to *Focus on the Family* and they gave their approval.

Now they have given me their permission to be on the radio broadcast. No one is doing more for the family than *Focus*, but Lord, I'm frightened. I don't want to compromise Angela, or do something that will not be good for her. If I can meet her needs and at the same time help other hurting parents, then I am willing to go.

Oh Father . . . may this help to bring restitution to Angela's heart so that she can see her failure has been forgiven and that You, God, are always faithful in exchanging beauty for ashes.

February 18

I have been encouraged by the church's continual support for Angela. Her repentant spirit and the evident change in her life has made it easier for the women to pour out their love and affection for her.

Joani has been sitting back watching all this take place, and I believe this is now creating a problem. The week Angela announced the pregnancy I told her, "Angela, you are going to get a lot of attention and you will have to understand that I have to make sure that your sisters also receive my love and equal attention. . . ."

Because the whole church is acting like "expectant parents" and are being loving and concerned, Joani is now feeling left out. She has decided she "doesn't like church." The youth leaders are spending time trying to help Angela, so Joani also feels left out at the youth group.

Last night she said, "Dad, can I go spend the rest of the year at Grandma's . . . at least until the baby is born?"

It's hard. Where is the fine line between helping and encouraging the one who has fallen without making it appear to the world at large that, "Boy, it's worth it to sin . . . look at all the attention you get."

Lord, help me to give equal attention to all my children. Grant the church people insight as they strive to meet the needs of one another.

Meet the needs in Joani's life. Help her to see the real cost of Angela's sin. Even though she is forgiven, memories will always be a part of her life. Help Joani see that she has much to be thankful for. She has remained pure in her witness. I guess I'm just praying for an open heart to understand these things when I talk to her.

Lord, it's getting closer and closer to the time. I know I couldn't function every day unless You lived in my heart.

February 19

It is only one month to the expected arrival of my "momentary grandchild."

In the beginning, one of the questions haunting me has been "How will my daughter's coming baby affect my job?" Very few stopped attending church because "the preacher has a pregnant daughter."

Yesterday I went before the board who serve as overseers of the church planting organization I serve. I told them I was ready to conclude the work of establishing my present new church so they could begin looking for the first permanent minister.

I'm supposed to start another church, but I am empty and I just do not have the strength to begin again. I explained this to the board and stated that I wanted to continue with the organization if they would give me a change in job description for a period of time. I feel exhausted. I need rest. I certainly need wisdom.

To begin the tremendous task of building a church from scratch requires a full-time commitment and a homefront with the normal amount of problems. To move from the security of friends and a familiar church family to start all over again seems an insurmountable task at this point. It means finding a place to meet, getting things like song books, piano, and pulpit, and of course finding teachers and elders. Just the thought of all that wearies me. How good it has been to have ones to greet you when you arrive at church, and cheer you when you are discouraged, and weep with you when your heart is breaking. Oh Lord, I just can't begin all over again right now. My faith is not strong enough.

Lord, right now I'm a sheep . . . I need a shepherd. Please continue the healing of my heart and home so I can get back to the job of being a shepherd of Your precious flock.

February 22

The family slept in a bit this morning and enjoyed a late breakfast together. We talked about the baby's birth and all the needed preparation. Suddenly Angela had enough, "I don't want anyone's help!"

"Well, I just won't help then," Joani snapped back. "She can ask one of her friends to help her . . . I'm *only* her sister."

Bobbi and I confronted Angela because of her attitude. She said, "Well, she wasn't there when I needed her!"

The same old conflict continues to hurt us all . . . Angela still has not forgiven Joani.

I believe Angela is still tortured in her heart and that she will continue to be until she finally forgives. Her continued failure to forgive Joani is harming everyone in the family.

Lord, help her to learn "to whom much is given much will be required." Help forgiveness to be complete so she can forgive herself.

February 25

A friend asked me the other day what advice I would give about raising children.

I told him that I had read in a book one time that if you want to have happy children, love your children's mother well.

I continued, "I believe one of the reasons we've coped as well as we have through this current crisis is that we had already, as a couple, faced the issue of teen pregnancy. We had role-played what we would do if one of our four daughters became pregnant."

I don't want you to think that we feared one of them would become pregnant . . . we just knew that there is tremendous pressure on teens, and they might not always keep their eyes on Jesus.

"Daddy, I'm Pregnant!"

Just what would our Heavenly Father do if He heard the words "Father, I'm pregnant." On one of our weekly times alone together, Bobbi and I discussed what we thought the Lord's reaction would be. We could envision his quiet voice, his open arms reaching out to the confessing sinner. We could see love extending from the heavens to surround the fallen one. How could we be any different?

On the night I heard those words I was able to carry out what I had already given much thought to. God's grace was able to reach through me to my precious brokenhearted daughter, and there was not one moment, not one breath, before she heard my expression of love filled with sorrow.

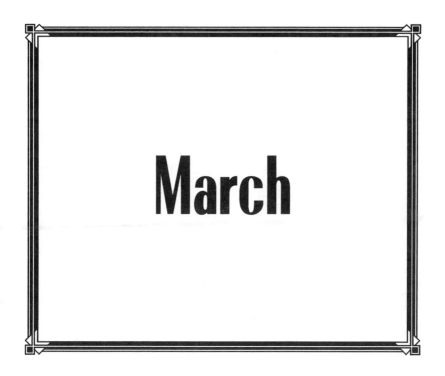

March

March 2

The month of March is here. The baby could come any day. The whole family is exhausted but we're hanging together, supporting each other, especially Angela.

Bobbi and I have experienced real harmony throughout the nine months, but I feel even closer to her as the birth draws near.

Our other daughters have been getting along and our home is ready emotionally for the baby.

Angela is not large by most standards so the baby will be about five pounds. This will make the birth easier, so we're told.

We have been in contact with the lawyer of the adoptive parents and everything is ready. Our go-between will come to the hospital and take the baby to the adoptive parents who will be waiting close by.

I'm so glad that I organized a revival meeting for our home church during this week of waiting. Having my best minister friend here in our home — to share with the church, to help with any counseling — has really helped. All of our family has enjoyed having him with us, and the week has really gone by quickly.

It's wonderful to realize that a year ago, when the meeting was arranged, God knew we would need special help and encouragement *this* very week.

I'm so grateful that God is able to see all of the future and He is so loving that He provides for our needs even before we know we have a need.

March — Due Date

I thought that by now I'd be emotionally ready to give that little baby into someone else's home, but I'm not. I'm lonesome for a little bundle of life I don't even know.

Lord, please fill my empty spot. I must be strong to help my daughter fulfill the decision she and Dan have made. Help me remember that You, God, are a God of constant love and that You will never leave the child nor forsake it. You really don't need me to hold the child, You don't need me to give the child stability and love. Remind me Lord, that even out of confusion and crisis You can bring something beautiful.

Lord, this is the day I've looked forward to. Today is the day the doctor gave for the baby's birth. My sweet little Angela has grown so large and uncomfortable. Being the father of five, I know that babies come when they are ready, regardless of anyone's predictions, including the doctor's.

Lord, only You know the arrival time of this tiny child . . . please keep my Angela safe as she has her baby.

March 11

When our children were born, Bobbi and I didn't have to go through the waiting game of counting the date plus one, plus two, plus three, plus four days. Our five were all born early or on time.

Waiting . . . if only they had waited to share sexually until marriage. . . . If they had waited until they had God's blessing, then we might be waiting for daughter Joani to come home from visiting a friend, or we might be playing some silly table game.

Lord, please help me to be patient. Remind me that learning to wait on You always proves best. It is so easy to want to run ahead. Draw Angela and Dan close to You so they will be ready for the coming baby.

March — Birth Day

The day we have longed for has arrived. Bobbi and I picked up Angela from school for her scheduled doctor's appointment. On the way she told us she had experienced "stomach cramps" at school. When Bobbi mentioned this to the doctor he sent us off to the hospital. So off to the races we went!

The doctor put Angela on a monitor to see if she was indeed in labor, and about 6:00 P.M. the nurse confirmed the fact that we were indeed about to have a baby. While Bobbi waited with Angela, Melissa stood by to hold me up; I was grateful for her comfort and love. We called Dan and his parents and waited. The cramps soon turned to pains and about 7:15 P.M. Dan and his parents arrived at the hospital.

I will never forget the kindness and love shown by Dan. That fifteen-year-old boy entered the room and for the next three hours held her hand, hugged her, wiped away tears (hers and his own), and made a very difficult time a bit easier. That quiet young man, who says so very little, proved himself to us all. I told him afterwards, "Dan, the way you've acted over the last months and the way you treated Angela tonight . . . you've made up for everything and I'm proud to know you."

Bobbi was a tower of strength, and I was a basket case. She coached and I cried. She stood in the gap, and I created gaps. It was a very difficult night. Watching my little daughter endure pain . . . realizing that out of this pain would come emptiness rather than a grandchild to hold. About 10:30 P.M., after several hours of heavy labor, Angela gave birth to a beautiful baby daughter.

Dan stood quietly in the hall. After Angela was returned to her room, he had a chance to see her. He came out into the hall, leaned against the wall, and sighed, "I think I'm going to make it. I didn't think I would for a while."

I understood Dan's feelings. Many times in the last nine months I've wondered if I would make it.

March 18

Sleep came hard last night. I dreaded the morning. I knew that soon I would be holding my tiny granddaughter. The thought of giving her up was tearing me apart.

We arrived at the hospital to hear that the baby and mother had rested well, but that they had discovered a heart murmur in the baby. "Don't worry," we were told.

I snuggled that tiny bundle in my arms . . . she was beautiful. I glanced up at Angela, she looked so very young and vulnerable. We took some pictures. Oh God, how can I say goodbye?

Afternoon came and I had to leave the hospital to minister at a funeral. I returned immediately to learn that the baby's heart murmur had become a flutter. The adoptive family visited very late and fell in love with our baby.

Bobbi decided to stay overnight in the room with Angela and I went home to be with the other two girls.

The next morning I taught my class at the college and then went to the hospital. The baby had worsened, and an emergency team had been called from a nearby hospital. They transferred the baby to a facility where she could receive special help.

She was so tiny and so distressed. Her little heart was beating so fast that it frightened us all. We woke up Angela and together we went to see the baby for the last time. They were putting tubes into her and getting her ready for transport. We stood weeping, and in my heart I was just sure that soon, very soon, I would have a granddaughter in heaven.

Angela collapsed. I think it was from the shock of the whole ordeal, so we waited to make sure she was all right before we took her home.

All day we tried to keep our minds off that little bundle in critical care. Angela wanted me to tell Dan that she was home from the hospital, so I drove over to the school to let him know.

It was Dan's sixteenth birthday. What a way to spend your sixteenth birthday! Your girlfriend has just arrived home from the hospital; your child is in critical care and may die. That young man has shown me more courage and character than I ever possessed as a sixteen-year-old boy.

March 19

The doctor called about 3:00 P.M. They are hoping the baby has a defective aorta. If the aorta is impaired, they can do surgery and the baby has a good chance.

If it is not the aorta the baby will not live. Between 6:00 and 8:00 P.M. they will do an echogram. It will help determine the cause of the great distress in the baby.

6:00 P.M. The hospital called. It appears that she has a defective aorta. If the baby can make it though the night, they will inject dye into her heart to locate the difficulty and determine if it is operable.

Hope! — The very thing we needed most. Maybe the baby will be all right.

What About the Adoptive Parents?

The biggest crisis right now is not Angela. She will survive and go on with her life. It is not the baby. If she dies she will go to be with Jesus. The ache in my heart right now is for the adoptive parents. They were chosen with much care. The kids selected them out of many who wanted the baby. This dear couple, who have experienced multiple miscarriages, now face the real possibility of losing the baby they so desperately want. They also face tremendous financial obligations.

Bobbi and I decided to call our minister friend go-between. We wanted him to contact the couple's lawyer. We wanted the couple to know that if for any reason, emotional or financial, they could not accept the baby, we would take her back. We had not changed our minds about the adoption; we still feel it is in the best interest of the baby. We called because we wanted the adoptive couple to know that we understand if they needed to change their minds.

The word came back through our minister go-between that this dear couple already thought of the baby as their own. They named her Ashley. What a pretty name for a pretty baby.

Lord, bless this special couple. We will make it if the baby dies. If the baby worsens, she will go to heaven to be with You. But Lord, this couple needs a blessing. Help us to be sensitive to their needs.

March 20

Today is the day they will test Ashley to see if surgery will help her. They will be using a heart catheter and dye test to see if the problem is an undeveloped heart, or if the problem is in the aorta.

I stayed home today to answer the phone and care for Angela. As Ashley's mother, it was up to Angela to make the final decision regarding surgery; this weighed heavily upon her. Many have called assuring us of their prayers. A minister friend came by to help. One of the church families brought us supper. We could not have managed without this support.

As I sit here and wait for the hospital to call, I'm thinking of that wonderful adoptive family waiting at the hospital. I wish I could be there to support them. I am so grateful for our go-between, Steve. He has ministered to them in a special way.

Waiting is so difficult. But wait we must. I've asked Bobbi to come home from work early and get a nap. Angela is sleeping.

The hospital finally called. They will do surgery tomorrow. Ashley has four major heart defects — any one of which would be considered major surgery. Her chances are not good.

I checked with our go-between to see if the adoptive family would allow us to be at the hospital during the surgery. They lovingly said yes, so we will remain on the first floor and they will be on the surgery floor.

I've called every friend and family member I can get hold of to ask them to pray.

Our church is going to have a prayer meeting during the surgery. I've asked the people not to go to the hospital. We don't want the adoptive family to feel pressure of any kind.

It's night. Angela can't sleep. She's afraid. Bobbi is sleeping with her.

March 21

Dan and his mother came over to ride with us to the hospital. We stopped for breakfast and arrived at the scheduled surgery time. The wait began at 10:30 A.M.

At 12:30 our go-between told us the doctor had just talked with the adoptive family and would soon come down and report to us. His report was grim . . . Ashley was inoperable. Her little aorta was not even large enough to be attached to the heart and lung machine for surgery.

The surgeon came and said there was nothing they could do to give Ashley a normal life.

I called our family and the church prayer chain again with the news that we expect Ashley to go to be with Jesus.

About an hour later another surgeon, a cardiologist, came and said that he had one suggestion. He could try an angioplasty. This would mean inserting a special instrument into her artery, moving it past the heart valve to the problem area to try to use a little balloon to expand the small aorta. It is a normal procedure for adults but has never been tried on an infant.

I asked him, "If this was your baby, what would you do?"

"I would go ahead," he replied, "and then I would take her off life support systems and let God decide whether or not she was supposed to live."

Angela and Dan, Bobbi and I and Dan's mother all agreed to proceed. Steve, our go-between, went to find the adoptive family to see what they wanted to do. They wanted to think and pray about this, so the decision would be made in the morning.

It is now 8:00 A.M. We called the hospital and they said Ashley was beginning to wake from yesterday's anesthetic. She is down to 50 percent oxygen. That's good.

The adoptive family should be arriving at the hospital soon. I'm very nervous. What if they decide against the surgery? Will we have to proceed in spite of them? We are in deep trouble. The pressure on all of us is mounting and at times we feel overwhelmed.

Again I remind myself of all the prayers of God's people. I also remind myself that God's eternal purpose will be done and I ask Him for a special portion of His strength for this day.

I feel that God has said "no" about Ashley, but "yes" to all of us involved. He is here! I thank Him so.

March 22

Bobbi just walked into the room and said "Why?"

I don't have an answer.

Our friend's daughter played basketball right up to two weeks before her baby was born, and her baby is normal. One of the kids at school is on drugs and alcohol and her baby is normal. Angela did everything the doctor asked her to do. She exercised, walked to school, didn't baby herself and didn't even miss one day of school. She ate the right foods, rested as the doctor asked, did exercises, refused to even take aspirin . . . and yet we have a sick baby. *Why?*

Lord, You sure have Your hands full trying to help us figure this one out. I wish I could call heaven and get an answer. In the Bible You say in Psalm 139 that "You form the baby from the womb." I believe that once the parents put in their part with the sperm and egg, You take that contribution with its inherited weaknesses and traits and You, Father, build a baby. Why did You allow this baby to be defective? How can You receive glory from this circumstance? I know You are in the middle of this crisis. I feel Your peace of mind, Your help in dealing with every decision, but why?

Why? I don't know. I told Angela, "Sis, we don't have to understand *why* to know that God loves us. Have you felt his help every day along the way?"

"Yes."

"Do you know God loves you?"

"Yes."

"I guess we will just have to ask God why when we get to heaven, don't you suppose?"

Lord, all I can say is please help me face today and what I'm sure is coming.

March 23

Last night we had prepared to turn baby Ashley over to the Lord. After the doctor's report, we felt it best to begin to withdraw all life support systems. If Ashley lives, it will be because she is supposed to. If she dies, it is because the Lord wants her at home in heaven. We went to bed last night expecting that by Monday she would be in heaven.

Sunday morning was difficult . . . but we all went to church together. Brother Jim preached for me, and the people were wonderful. It is so good to have all the kids home with us.

Sunday night the doctor called and said, "The baby is off life support and she is doing well . . . the adoptive family want to try the angioplasty procedure." We called Dan and his family, then called the doctor back and said "Go for it."

Angela cried. She wanted the baby . . . did anyone really understand how much?

She wanted "her" Ashley, but she knew she couldn't take care of her. She wanted to meet the adoptive family hoping she wouldn't like them so she could keep Ashley. But having met the family and seeing them with the baby, seeing their love for Ashley, she now found herself wanting them to have Ashley too. What tremendous pressure for a fifteen year old.

She tried to explain to Dan just how important it was for her that Ashley knew she was loved. He had tried to reason with her. It would have been wiser for him to just say, "Yes, it's hard for me too," but he didn't. Only kids themselves . . . how could they possibly meet each other's needs?

Bobbi slept with Angela again last night. I sure thank God for my wife and her constant love.

March 24

The doctor still has not called to tell us about the angio-plasty procedure. He should have called! The nurse said the baby had a bad night. She didn't sound hopeful.

We have not talked to the doctor or to Dan's parents today. I know that God is on the job.

Angela is better today. Bobbi is not. She is showing signs of wear, and so I'm glad she can go to work for a few hours and get away from the pressure.

It's 3:00 P.M. Finally the doctor called. We had waited all day. We thought that the procedure had been done in the morning, but it had not.

The doctor said that the procedure would be done immediately and he would call us back within two hours. He said that he hoped to have a healthier baby after the surgery.

I told him that the baby was not ours or the adoptive family's but it was God's, and that we only asked him to do his best and let God do the rest. I asked him to tell the adoptive family that we love them and that we would be praying for the doctor. He replied, "I'm going right now to say a little prayer myself."

5:40 P.M. The doctor called. The procedure was not successful. When Ashley became distressed he ceased the process. He says they are taking her off of the medication and we will now wait and see if she will live. It's up to the Lord. Everything we can do has been done. We now wait.

Two things stand out in my mind.

When we arrived at the hospital and my brother Jim arranged for us to meet the adoptive family for the first time, Angela and Dan didn't want to see them. So the four parents were ushered into a small room. Two red-eyed lovely people entered the room and we wept together. "Our Ashley" had made us one.

Bobbi and I went down to be with the kids. Angela asked if she could see Ashley for the last time. As Angela, Bobbi, and I entered the baby intensive care, we caught a quick glimpse of Ashley and her adoptive parents through the window. We stood there for a moment, not wanting to disturb. The beautiful young woman looked up and saw us. She rushed out of the room toward us.

"Are you Angela?" Before Angela could answer, she threw her arms around her and said, "Angela, oh, Angela, thank you . . . thank you. You have given me the most wonderful gift that anyone could ever give." Imagine, God used this woman whose arms would also soon be empty to bring comfort and healing to my daughter!

I just fell apart. Finding an empty room, I wept. I will remember that scene for the rest of my life.

Oh God, I sobbed, *a beautiful baby . . . so precious . . . is just passing through our lives. We will never be the same.*

March 25

Ashley took her first breath in heaven today. She lived for seven days. Lord, we need You now. How are we going to go on?

How do we answer our hearts when our hearts cry out, "Why, God?" There seemed to be such a perfect solution to this whole tragedy. A perfect couple for our little Ashley.

Guide in spite of my feelings. Make me numb, so I can cope with the next few days. And then, Lord, thaw me out slowly to keep me from falling apart. Help me to be a witness even though I don't have answers. May I continually remember Your Word.

Psalm 23:4 "Even though I walk through the valley of the shadow of death, I will fear no evil, for you are with me."

Psalm 116:15 "Precious in the sight of the LORD is the death of his saints."

Later the same day

Too many people . . . too much emotion . . . too many questions. We gathered in a small room at the funeral home to make the necessary preparations. As I looked around the room — seeing the adoptive parents, my family, Dan's mother, Steve — I couldn't help but sense that we still had but one question: "Why, Lord?"

Bobbi's Uncle Earl is the funeral director. This we see as another evidence of God's provision. I wonder if we could have made it without his help. He showed such kindness to us all. He controlled the hour spent together and because of his professionalism and kind Christian spirit we all experienced healing.

There will be two funerals. One here where her birth parents can share with friends and family. The adoptive family will have their own service. The baby will be buried there,

85

and we will not attend. We both need to claim Ashley as our own and have our own private goodbyes.

Angela and Dan selected a small pink casket. Bobbi and Dan's mother chose the flowers.

Uncle Earl provided as a gift of love the expenses for the funeral. Friends and family shared financially to cover the other expenses involved in Ashley's homegoing.

Lord, tonight I'm thinking of Angela's empty arms. Please surround her with Your love and help her through tomorrow. It's going to be a very difficult day. I'm almost empty beyond words.

March 26

People began to gather for the service — family, friends from all over the state. The chapel soon filled. Our special friend, Keith, sang a song he had written for Angela and Ashley; Steve shared from the Scriptures and my brother Rex stood and read what I'd written in loving memory of Ashley.

From the moment her coming was announced, Ashley only knew love. She was loved by her birth parents. Two very young kids who met and over a period of two years fell in love. They followed their heart instead of their faith, and Ashley was on her way into the world.

From the moment Ashley's pregnancy was announced she was only shown love by her birth mother. Doing just what the doctor ordered, exercising, not missing a single day of school, resting — all this so the coming child would be healthy.

She was loved by her birth parents. You would have known Ashley was loved as you watched that fourteen-year-old girl and that fifteen-year-old boy accept their responsibility. If you could have watched them stand together, make difficult decisions together, make every effort to determine what was best for Ashley . . . you would have known she was loved. To listen to the phone calls in the night as those two kids talked about what was best: Should they marry? Should they keep the coming baby? Should they find a couple to open their hearts and adopt the coming baby? To watch those kids make the decision that they were too young to marry, that they should pray for a couple to love Ashley, to see the pain in their lives as they decided which family would be selected . . . yes, Ashley was loved.

To watch those two kids share the pains of the coming child, to see their joy at the correct number of fingers and toes, to see their concern as the baby showed signs of illness, to see their pain and confusion over the baby getting sicker, to see their mixed emotions over the fact that they wanted that kind couple to have a healthy baby. To see Ashley's birth parents' heartbreak over her going home to heaven. Yes, the birth parents loved Ashley very much . . . they always will.

Ashley was loved by her birth grandparents. Four strangers who met seven months ago to deal with their teenagers. Those strangers learned to care for each other and to support each other. That little baby, so small and frail, was truly loved by its birth grandparents. Ashley, the first grandchild. Our arms are empty but our hearts are full.

Ashley was loved by friends. The kindness of the church, the helpfulness of friends who served as taxi or brought food or shared with cards or phone calls, those who helped financially — all proved again that Ashley was loved. These friends who drove over to support the adoptive parents, those who fed and housed them while they were here loving Ashley. Truly Ashley was surrounded by people who showed her love.

Ashley only knew love from her adoptive family. Adoption means in the Bible "a child placed." Truly God led in the selection of the adoptive parents. No two people could have opened their hearts more than this wonderful man and wife. We have watched them love Ashley with all their precious selves. We have watched their kindness and understanding. I believe that God answered our prayer for someone to come and help us love Ashley.

Ashley was surrounded by love at the hospitals. The kindness of each doctor, each nurse, each support person. Truly she only knew love from these wonderful, caring people.

Ashley only knew love from her extended family. Aunts and uncles, grandparents and great-grandparents, the friends of her three families surrounded her with love.

We don't understand. We do not know why God allowed this bundle of blessing to be with us so briefly. We know that we are much richer for having our hearts stretched. We now send her on to God. He will care for her. He will heal her heart. He will heal our hearts. We do not understand, but we trust. We trust God that He knows what is best for Ashley.

Ashley, you were in our hearts for nine months, in our arms for one brief week, and now you will be in our hearts for the rest of our lives. You were only with us for a brief time, but in that short week you were surrounded by enough love to fill a lifetime. Ashley, because you're now in heaven, it makes heaven just a little sweeter. We want you to know that we love you, you touched our lives, and we will never be the same.

Ashley . . . you are loved!

Nine Months Later

December 31

Tonight closes out the year. I think it was the best-worst year of my entire life.

Last year began with Angela's pregnancy. We had no idea what the coming year would bring. We faced it with sober thoughts and a lot of questions. A year later we have some answers.

Our family has held together. We have weathered the storm. The Lord took the baby home to heaven. We survived. Not just survived, we were victorious! The Lord be praised and honored!

What happened to Dan? The boy just slipped out of our lives and sometimes we miss him. We won't forget him, and we are grateful for the time he stood by us. We pray that someday he will find Jesus as his Lord and Savior.

At times I find myself flooded with resentment and bitterness over the bills that face us. I try to remind myself that Bobbi and I agreed to assume Ashley's huge medical debt knowing there would be no help from our insurance. The insurance would not cover Ashley's expenses because she was Angela's child and not ours. So far, Dan's parents have only felt able to send a token of the expense, and it is doubtful that we should expect anything in the future. And Bobbi and I feel that if the adoptive family is ever to adopt another child they have to be clear of this expense. Oh how we want them to have a child to fill their empty arms.

When I become too discouraged, my sweetheart Bobbi reminds me of all the blessings of the past year:

Our granddaughter is in heaven.

We have experienced God's daily help.

Our love is deeper and our marriage is stronger than before.

Our son Jim has a deeper relationship with Christ and has found a Christian girl to share his dreams. He hopes to someday be in the ministry.

Melissa will marry this summer. What a joy! Both she and her future husband are wanting to serve God.

Joani and Angela have become best of friends.

Joani is blossoming into a fine young woman. She hopes to attend Bible college this fall. The pressure of this last year turned that small bit of sand in her life into a beautiful pearl.

Melody, our youngest, is a blessing to us all.

And Angela . . . dear Angela, she still faces uncertain days and often retreats into herself. But God took this unhappy little girl who had taken her eyes off the Lord and He gently restored her to himself. Angela, we have her back. She makes us laugh until we cry . . . She shares her fears openly now . . . She cries with us when she misses Ashley. She reminds us that we have so much to be thankful for, and therefore we have so much hope for the tomorrows.

Lord, the future is unknown to me. But knowing You hold the future is enough. My faith in You is not a blind faith based upon emotions alone, it is a faith based upon my confidence in Your Word because Your Word always proves true! You have kept Your Word; You have been faithful even when I haven't. You have allowed me to bend without breaking, to lose without being defeated. You have allowed my children to see me at my weakest. You have chosen to use me in spite of my failures.

I am reminded of the beautiful passage in Isaiah 61:1-6 where I discovered again that God indeed brings Good News to the afflicted because He brought it to me. He binds up the brokenhearted because He bound up my broken heart. He set the captive free because He freed me of my sin. He makes this a favorable year, and He brings forth a garland out of the ashes of my life. He brings gladness into my mourning heart and praise into my failing heart. He makes me to stand like a giant oak in the storm of life. He rebuilds the ruins of my life and allows me to be called His priest.

Lord, I find myself writing the last entry of my journal for the year. New beginnings lie ahead and as always the future is not known. So once again I bow my head and commit myself to Your safe keeping for yet another year. And just one more thing, Lord . . . please kiss little Ashley for me. You used her to teach me so much.

Three Years Later

Hi! I'm Angela.

At the end of my dad's journal, I just wanted to add this letter and share some things with you. Often when I read a book, I wonder what has happened to the people in the story. A few years have passed since this story's events, and in that time I've learned some special lessons. May I share them with you?

If you are a parent of a pregnant girl, please be loving and forgiving. Your daughter feels very alone and scared, and she needs all the love you can give her. I don't know what I would have done without my parents' support.

If you're a friend of a pregnant girl, try to be a REAL friend. She needs your understanding and encouragement. I have a very special friend named Tammy who was always there for me no matter what. She encouraged me and didn't treat me differently as some of my other friends did. I could never have made it through the long school year without Tammy.

And finally, if you are a pregnant girl, I know you are tired of people saying they know what you're going through. They may mean well, but they don't really understand. Well, I can honestly say that I know what you are going through. We chose to love a guy more than we loved God, to trust the words of a guy and not God's Word, so we fell flat on our faces; now we can choose to move forward to make things right.

Two verses that have helped me are Romans 8:28, "We know that God causes all things to work together for good to those who love God," and Philippians 4:13, "I can do all things through Him who strengthens me." Trust God and He will never let you down or betray you. I find real comfort in knowing He is ALWAYS there and that He can make good come out of failure and disappointment.

When I first found out I was pregnant, I immediately decided to get an abortion, but then I realized I could never live with the guilt because I believe abortion is wrong. If you're pregnant, please think long and hard about what you will do to your baby. Don't let your boyfriend or your friends or anyone persuade you to do wrong. Look to God for guidance and you will find it.

I thank you for reading my story. I hope that it has helped you in some way. All the hard times will be worth it if someone comes to know the Lord or is encouraged by this book.

I also want to thank my family for being my best friends and for helping me to pick up the broken pieces. I want to thank Tammy for being my best buddy. My church was there when I needed them — I'm so grateful. I want to thank God for His forgiveness and love. And most of all, I thank Him for Ashley. Although I only had her for a short time I will never forget her. Ashley will be in my heart and in Jesus' arms forever.

Love, Angela

Thirteen Years Later

Dear Angela,

From the girl you were to the woman you have become;
From those months of rebellion to your years of faithfulness;
From those months of tears to the years of laughter and joy;
From those moments of embarrassment to the years of pride;
From those months of selfishness to your years of serving;
From who you were to who you have become,

MOM AND I ARE SO PROUD OF YOU!

Because of your courage to take your broken heart to the Lord and allow Him to heal you and to then allow your story to be told, thousands have been touched. They have not been touched by your months of failure but by your years of faithfulness. Thousands of parents have been given hope because of the change you allowed the Lord to make in you. The hundreds of babies that have been kept from death because of your story . . . Thank you! You are a treasure to me and to our family.

Sis, because you allowed me to share in your healing, I was able to be a better dad to you through the crisis than I had before. Thank you! The memories we share of how God worked in our lives are some of the greatest treasures I have in life. Thank you for being my daughter and my friend.

Dear Reader,

Many people have asked WHAT HAPPENED TO THE PEOPLE MENTIONED IN THE BOOK:

- ❖ Angela confessed her sin and allowed the Lord to forgive her. How she lived her life proved her repentance was genuine.
- ❖ As you read, the Lord *began* to make wonderful changes in our family.
- ❖ When our first granddaughter Ashley died, the boy left us and we have lost contact with him.
- ❖ With our granddaughter Ashley's death, we were left with thousands of dollars in uninsured medical bills. The Lord gave His grace and He paid off the entire amount in just *seven* years.
- ❖ The adoptive family who went home with empty arms had their arms filled within two years with one child by adoption and one by birth.

Where we are now:

- ❖ Bobbi and I are still serving the Lord in the ministry of planting new churches. We enjoy teaching what we have learned about God's grace and how the church is to love broken people while the Lord is changing them.

❖ Our son is serving in full-time ministry with his wife and three children. Sometimes the memory of his childhood anger and abusiveness comes back to haunt me and remind me of our failure as father and son, but watching the change God has been making in his life, and the godly fruits I see in him over ten consistent years is teaching me that God can truly bring conversion to repentant sinners and use them to help people find the Lord.

❖ Our oldest daughter worked to put her husband through college and in between having children, she received her teaching degree. She is in full-time ministry with her husband and two children. As we watch her constant concern for her siblings, her mother and me, the Lord is teaching me through her what true friendship is like and how the Lord uses people to build bridges to restored relationships.

❖ Our next daughter is married to a man in the military and they have one daughter named "Ashley." Of all my children, she was the most hurt by the failures in our home. As I watch her life and how she deals with the painful memories of her childhood, the Lord is using her to teach me that, "forgetting is impossible, true forgiveness is very costly, but forgiveness is possible only with the Lord's help. As she supports her husband and his career at the cost of her own dreams and ambitions, I learn all over again, true love gives.

❖ Our daughter Angela launched herself into serving God and gaining an education. She and her husband are in full-time ministry and she is a teacher. God is using her to teach me that, "*after* God forgives, God restores." His forgiveness and restoration can bring us a wonderful life and productiveness. She illustrates over and over to me that "we can't go back, but because of Jesus Christ we can start over."

❖ Our youngest daughter is married to an EMT/nurse and they have two children. She is caring for her family and preparing herself for special needs people. As I watch her life, God is teaching me the meaning of true commitment. There is nothing that she and the Lord will not try. The last two years she was in my home I really was an "absentee father," so, I'm grateful that her Heavenly Father filled in for my failure and taught her she could trust in Him.

❖ My wife Bobbi continues to make my life complete. There is no other person in my life that has been so used by God to "calm my troubled heart." We now have eight living grandchildren, with more to come!

❖ Our five children have each brought home a wonderful mate that we love deeply. They have brought strength to our family, and the Lord is using them to bring love and continued healing to our children.

❖ Bobbi and I have been privileged to experience the grace and peace of God in such wonderful ways and to see our story of God's faithfulness shared by Focus on the Family five times; the 700 Club; The Art of Family Living, and many others. Nearly 30,000 copies of the original *Daddy I'm Pregnant* published by Multnomah Press have been read.

BUT IS THIS THE REST OF THE STORY?

Before you get the idea that all our problems are behind us, I want you to know that the past still jumps up to hurt us. So often I wish that I'd been a better father, and that we had raised our family in a godly, safe home. Even though the Lord has forgiven us, in our human frailty, we too often choose to review the past and we again feel pain. For just moments, we forget our failures or the failures of others. For moments we forgive others' failures but then we remember them all over again.

It is my prayer that you will learn the lesson that our family continues to learn, IT'S NOT THAT WE ARE A GREAT FAMILY . . . IT'S THAT WE HAVE A GREAT GOD! IT'S NOT THAT WE HAVE ARRIVED, BUT, *PRAISE GOD*, WE ARE ARRIVING! Some of our memories will not be healed this side of heaven, but day by day, memory by memory, the Lord is healing us as individuals and as a family. As you read our story, please know that I am praying for you and that I want you to pray for us as a family.

My prayer:

"Lord, I so often forget that I'm not a finished product! I look at my doubts and fears and I remember what I should have, or could have done, or what I shouldn't have done in the past and I hate me all over again. Lord, I wonder, How can You love me? How can my family love me? I look at my unfinished marriage or I sometimes look at my adult children and I forget that it's YOU who will make them prepared people for that prepared place.

"Lord, my words are so inadequate. If those who are reading this book are feeling like they are beyond help, please take the scales of self-pity from their eyes and help them see that if they are not Christians, You are waiting to begin construction in their lives. If they are Christians, please help them learn all over again that they are not finished products.

"Lord, thank You. Thank You for all You *did*, thank You for all You *are* doing, and thank You for all that You *will do*. I stand amazed that You are willing to make "something beautiful out of our lives."

In Christ,

A dad named Bill
29190 S. Dhooghe Road
Colton, Oregon 97017